T0158505

PENGUIN
SPECIALS

Penguin Specials fill a gap. Written by some of today's most exciting and insightful writers, they are short enough to be read in a single sitting – when you're stuck on a train; in your lunch hour; between dinner and bedtime. Specials can provide a thought-provoking opinion, a primer to bring you up to date, or a striking piece of fiction. They are concise, original and affordable.

To browse digital and print Penguin Specials titles, please refer to **penguin.com.au/penguinspecials**

LOWY INSTITUTE

The Lowy Institute is an independent, nonpartisan international policy think tank. The Institute provides high-quality research and distinctive perspectives on the issues and trends shaping Australia's role in the world. The Lowy Institute Papers are peer-reviewed essays and research papers on key international issues affecting Australia and the world.

For a discussion on *Xi Jinping: The Backlash* with Richard McGregor and leading commentators on China, visit the Lowy Institute's daily commentary and analysis site, *The Interpreter*: **lowyinstitute.org/the-interpreter/debate/xi-jinping-the-backlash**.

Richard McGregor is a Senior Fellow at the Lowy Institute and a leading expert on China's political system. He is an award-winning journalist and author. From 2000 to 2009 he was the *Financial Times* bureau chief in Beijing and Shanghai, and headed the Washington office for four years from 2011. Prior to joining the FT, he was the chief political correspondent and China and Japan correspondent for *The Australian*. His book *The Party: The Secret World of China's Communist Rulers* won numerous awards, including the Asia Society in New York award in 2011 for best book on Asia. His latest book, *Asia's Reckoning: China, Japan, and the Fate of US Power in the Pacific Century*, was described as 'shrewd and knowing' by *The Wall Street Journal*, and a 'compelling and impressive' read by *The Economist*, and in 2018 won the Prime Minister's Literary Award for Non-Fiction.

LOWY INSTITUTE

Xi Jinping:
The Backlash

A LOWY INSTITUTE PAPER

RICHARD McGREGOR

PENGUIN BOOKS

UK | USA | Canada | Ireland | Australia
India | New Zealand | South Africa | China

Penguin Books is part of the Penguin Random House group of companies
whose addresses can be found at global.penguinrandomhouse.com.

Penguin
Random House
Australia

First published by Penguin Books, 2019

Typeset by Midland Typesetters, Australia

Printed and bound in Australia by Griffin Press, part of Ovato, an accredited
ISO AS/NZS 14001 Environmental Management Systems printer

A catalogue record for this
book is available from the
National Library of Australia

ISBN 978 1 76089 304 0

penguin.com.au

MIX
Paper from
responsible sources
FSC® C009448

To Kath, Angus, Cate and Romeo

CONTENTS

Introduction

When did the world turn against China? It is hard to date precisely the moment the backlash against Xi Jinping and the party state in Beijing took hold. The construction, and then militarisation, of islands in the South China Sea from 2013 galvanised hawks in Washington and allies in the region, not least because of its sheer audacity and scale. Foreign businesses, once advocates of engagement with Beijing to open the Chinese market, became disillusioned when they saw their access truncated. The seemingly ceaseless theft of trade secrets and technology hardened cynicism in governments and companies alike. The detention of up to a million Uighurs in re-education camps in Xinjiang in the name of anti-terror from 2017 highlighted human rights abuses in a way the jailing of individual dissidents never could. Donald

Trump's election was a game changer by itself, as it gave cover to a broad-based coalition, bringing together America's rust belt, democracy activists and the deep state in Washington, all demanding a tougher line against Beijing. On the front line in Hong Kong, more than one million citizens took to the streets in June 2019 to protest against a proposed extradition law.

The contest between the United States and China, to take the prime battlefield, is multifaceted, including over ideology, technology, economics, trade and military superiority. Germany, by contrast, is focused not on military might but industrial competitiveness. Australia, like many countries in Asia, fears being left to fend for itself in a region unanchored by US power. Japan worries that China wants not just to dominate the seas surrounding it but settle historical scores as well. Taiwan, a self-governing island for decades, thinks it will be gobbled up, on terms dictated by Beijing. Singapore and Southeast Asian nations already feel marginalised in China's shadow. For Canada, the wake-up call came as late as December 2018, when Vancouver police detained a senior executive from the telco giant Huawei for extradition to the United States, only to see Beijing arrest Canadian citizens in China in retaliation and take them as virtual hostages.

However, if there is a period that crystallised perceptions of Xi, and his world view and ambitions, that moment was in late 2017 and early 2018 when foreigners, and many Chinese as well, finally started to take him at his word. Xi was reconfirmed as leader of the Chinese Communist Party in October 2017 and then abolished term limits on his presidency in March 2018, removing any obstacles to his remaining in power in perpetuity. On renewing his oath of office, he extolled the absolute leadership role of the Party to the exclusion of all other institutions. 'Government, military, society and schools, north, south, east and west – the Party is the leader of all,' Xi said at the opening of the once-every-five-years party congress in October 2017.[1] Unlike any Chinese leader of the reform era, Xi touted the virtues of Beijing's development model not just for China, but for other countries as well. China has always competed against democracy at home. Xi's promotion of what he called the 'China solution' suggested that it was girding itself for the same contest in defence of Beijing's growing interests abroad.

All the complaints that helped turn the tide overseas against China were familiar. Beijing has long had expansive claims in the South China Sea. Foreign businesses have struggled with barriers in the Chinese market since the country began opening up in the late 1970s. US, European and Japanese leaders have protested about the theft and transfer of technology for decades. Similarly, criticism of Chinese policies towards religious and ethnic groups, though principally focused on the treatment of Christians and Tibetans, is not new. But Xi's clarity of purpose provided a sharper lens through which the rest of the world could view China's actions. Not only had Beijing become more powerful and less willing to hide its disdain for its critics' views. Xi has articulated a willingness to leverage Beijing's elevated power to press the ruling communist party's ambitions with a force and coherence that his predecessors lacked.

There is another way of looking at the backlash against Xi, of course. To begin with, has the world turned against China, or is it just the United States and a few of its allies? China is more aligned with Russia than at any time in half a century and has forged close ties with multiple nations in Africa, as an investor in resources and builder of infrastructure. The Belt and Road Initiative, Beijing's vast political and economic plan to develop, fortify and dominate its hinterland and the sea routes connecting Europe, Eurasia and the Indian Ocean, is bringing new countries firmly into China's orbit, albeit not without problems. In March 2019, Xi signed Italy up to the Initiative, driving a political wedge into the top levels of the European Union itself. In the Pacific, Beijing has showered small island nations with attention and aid, inflating their bargaining power with their traditional benefactors, Australia and New Zealand. The United States and a handful of allies might be hanging up on Huawei and its advanced mobile technology but the rest of the world isn't. In addition, steadfast US allies such as Japan and Australia continue to sustain their economies through trading with China, even as they grow more wary of it.

Far from being high-minded, many see the US-led pushback against Beijing as about raw power, not as defending democracy. Indeed, senior Trump advisers don't demur from this analysis. 'This is not just an economic issue,' US National Security Advisor John Bolton stated. 'This is not just talking about tariffs and the terms of trade. This is a question of power.'[2] From the Chinese perspective, this is more than a good guys versus bad guys story. Rather, it is the last gasp of the US hegemon, struggling to maintain an order and hierarchy in Asia that is no longer sustainable. Even relatively liberal Chinese object to the US tactics to counter Beijing, such as the arrest of the Huawei executive, Meng Wanzhou. 'The arrest of Canadians was politically motivated? So was that of Meng,' tweeted Zhang Chunlin, an economist with the World Bank in Washington. '[The] difference? One side started this ugly game.'[3]

Beijing likes to call its critics hawks because it fits neatly with official propaganda that brands anyone contesting China's rise as being in the grip of 'Cold War thinking'. The term is as imprecise as it is misleading. Certainly, China hawks have always been among us, even at times of intense cooperation between Washington and Beijing over the Soviet Union in the 1970s and 1980s, and more recently under Barack Obama on climate change. But the truth is more unwieldy.

The loose coalition lining up against China is a motley bunch, spreadeagled across the world and straddling big business, academia, human rights activists, and the intelligence and defence establishments. Throw a few once idealistic China hands into the mix – the experts whose job used to be explaining Beijing's complexities to the world and who now increasingly warn loudest about its autocratic turn – and you get a sense of the distrust that has rapidly become mainstream. 'People I've known for decades have given up on China,' said Susan Shirk, an academic and official in Bill Clinton's administration with a lengthy engagement with China. 'There's a widespread view in the academic community that the overreaching China has done both domestically and internationally is hard-baked into the system and that there's no hope of getting them to adjust their behaviour to our interests and values.'[4]

There has never been a shortage of Westerners over centuries who claim to feel disappointed and let down by China. But this time the break seems sharper, and the divide greater. In the fracturing democratic political systems in the West, pushing back against China stands out as a rare issue that can garner bipartisan support. 'Hang tough on China,' Chuck Schumer, Democratic Senate leader and normally an avowed foe of the president, urged Trump in May 2019. 'Strength is the only way to win.'[5]

On one level, the intensity of the antagonism towards China is a puzzle. Xi's China is not Mao Zedong's China. The country is richer, more open economically, more educated and more intertwined with the world than the China that Mao ruled over ever was. China stands on the cusp of not just becoming the world's largest economy, but a technology and military superpower as well. The country's internet has become a byword for modernity as much as for the censorship that is often the focus of the foreign media. China's fast trains, airports and even highways are all dazzling feats of construction, especially for Westerners whose countries are benighted by ageing, substandard infrastructure. The country's technocrats are highly sophisticated, technically adept and often bilingual, and more than able to hold their own with policymakers in any other country.

Under Xi, however, China's politics have taken a different path. They have gone back in time, with echoes of the Maoist era, a period of ruthless purges, ideological education, loyalty tests and personality cults. The philosophy of 'Xi Jinping Thought' now permeates public life and education at all levels in China. In official propaganda, it operates as a catch-all phrase to animate everything from how to manage the economy to scholarly studies at universities. When China was challenged about human rights in Xinjiang at the United Nations in 2018, their officials defended the system by saying it was 'guided by Xi Jinping thought'.[6] Xi has not just re-energised the ideological state that Mao ruled over in a more primitive form. Under Xi, as with Mao, the personal is political as well.

Xi's ideological bent underpins the hardening foreign critique of China, of a hostile power more interested in surpassing the West than working with it. It also helps explain the reaction at home. The backlash against Xi inside China is less visible, for obvious reasons. Xi has made it perilous to oppose him openly. Even lofty members of the Politburo are careful to routinely pledge fealty, lest they fall foul of the leader. To be sure, Xi is in no danger of being toppled from his perch. As long as China's economy remains reasonably healthy, he can count on sufficient support to retain his hold on the system. But the anger towards Xi is potent nonetheless.

In July 2018, I spent two weeks in Beijing during which officials and scholars, party members and non-party members spoke unprompted about their fury at Xi and the direction he was taking the country. They complained about how he had stifled criticism, built up a cult of personality and mishandled relations with Washington. Initially, the critics kept their complaints underground. Later in 2018, some started to speak in public. 'Something strange is happening in Xi Jinping's China,' wrote Ian Johnson in *The New York Review of Books* in early 2019. In what was supposed to be the 'perfect dictatorship', the country was witnessing 'the most serious critique of the system in more than a decade, led by people inside China who are choosing to speak out now, during the most sensitive season of the most sensitive year in decades'.[7]

Xi faces an array of what we might call 'bad enemies' and 'good enemies', from the once rich and powerful families he destroyed in his anti-corruption campaign to the small-r reformers angered by his illiberal rollback of the incremental institutional advances of the reform period. Forced to lay low initially because of the dangers of challenging him outright, Xi's critics at home have begun to find their voice. They have been outspoken mainly on economic policy, but the deeper undercurrents of their criticisms are unmistakable. The sons of former top leaders, revered scholars who had guided China's economic miracle, frustrated private entrepreneurs and academics furious about Xi's unrelenting hard line all complain about Xi's policies and style.

Xi has for the moment scared off any organised opposition, but his ruthlessness has also caught him in a trap of his own making. Having unleashed the most far-reaching anti-corruption campaign in modern Chinese history, he has left himself with a perilously narrow off-ramp from office. Even with all the political and physical protection his current position offers, if he were to ever step down he knows that he, or at least his family and his close allies, would be vulnerable to being locked up by whomever came after him. Xi's supporters, paradoxically, mount a similar argument in defence of his abolition of term limits. They say that any successor nominated by Xi would be targeted by his enemies as a proxy to attack Xi and hobble his agenda. In a virtuosic display of circular logic, they maintain that the appointment of a successor would therefore cause instability, rather than the other way around.

It is true that many of Xi's policies mirror those of his predecessors, although backed by greater economic weight, diplomatic clout and military firepower. It is politics that sets Xi apart. Gradually, and then in a rush, Xi has ditched or unwound most if not all of the political advances that had been considered instrumental to modern China's success. Not only did Xi upend the system at home. Xi's China is now playing a different game abroad as well.

This is a story that runs along parallel and intersecting tracks; about China and the ruling communist party, and about Xi Jinping and the reaction to his politics at home and abroad. This paper will examine in detail two areas of policy that have dominated Xi's rule. First, the anti-corruption campaign, as well as the Party's relationship with the economy, particularly state and private business. Then it will look at a select number of countries and their response to the China challenge.

This paper is also about more than one man and the political party he heads. Today's China is not just a geopolitical challenge to the West. It is a real-time, empirical experiment challenging the West's post–Cold War ascendancy. Far from being a pre-modern throwback to discredited authoritarian ways, Xi's project is taking shape as a post-modern phenomenon, a surveillance state with a fighting chance of success at home and the potential to replicate its core elements abroad.

If Xi, and whomever takes over from him eventually, does manage to sustain the system, China will have decisively rebuffed any notions that democracy is the sole system capable of building a successful, rich country. This is not so much the end of the end of history. Xi's China marks the start of history all over again.

CHAPTER ONE

Panic stations

Soon after taking over as leader of the Chinese Communist Party in late 2012, Xi Jinping travelled to Shenzhen, near Hong Kong. Now China's equivalent to Silicon Valley as the home of many of the country's high-tech giants, Shenzhen occupies a near-mythical status in Chinese politics. Former paramount leader Deng Xiaoping chose the city as China's first staging post for the market economy in 1980 and returned there in 1992, a trip that marked an inflection point in modern China. Struggling to push back against anti-market conservatives, Deng's 'southern tour' was a pivotal moment that revitalised political support for the entrepreneurial economy. Xi's Shenzhen trip was inevitably interpreted through the same rose-coloured lens. Later, his visit would be conflated with a statement issued after a central committee conclave in November 2013, a meeting of senior leaders from government, business and the military, about how Xi's China would allow the market to play a 'decisive' role in the economy.[8]

Xi's energy and freshness were enough for seasoned commentators to lurch headlong into the narrative that has long blighted foreign analysis of modern China. Nicholas Kristof, the garlanded *New York Times* columnist and the paper's former Beijing correspondent, wrote that the new Chinese leader would 'spearhead a resurgence of economic reform, and probably some political easing as well'. He went on: 'Mao's body will be hauled out of Tiananmen Square on his watch, and Liu Xiaobo, the Nobel Peace Prize-winning writer, will be released from prison.'[9] Liu died in 2017, a month after being granted medical parole for liver cancer, and Mao's corpse remains undisturbed in his purpose-built mausoleum. It might seem like a cheap shot to drag up a columnist's past musings. Their job is to provoke and predict, which inevitably means they trip up. The point is not that Kristof was wrong, but that he fell into the trap that so many foreigners have wandered into for decades, of confusing Western beliefs about how China should reform with the Party's own convictions about how to govern the country.

The gushing over 'Xi the reformer' was one reason that many missed the real message Xi transmitted in Shenzhen. In part, this was because the most important speech of his trip was delivered in secret, and not leaked until later. Nonetheless, Xi's southern tour was, in retrospect, more a ritualistic feint than a conscious signal that he was setting off on a steady-as-she-goes Dengist path of incremental market reforms for the economy.

Rather, Xi did something completely different on coming to office: he pressed the panic button. The series of rapid-fire decisions that Xi took early in his tenure will reverberate for years, if not decades, in Chinese politics. Xi's decisions left big questions in their wake, including the extent to which they will blow back on him personally.

Chinese Communist Party leaders have always thrived on a liberal dose of paranoia. The Party system, after all, doesn't just exist on its own. It operates in opposition to something else: the West and democracy. The ever-present 'hostile foreign forces', as they are called, exist in two dimensions, intimately related. One is in the realm of history, and China's shame at being humiliated and dismembered by Western colonial powers and Japan from the mid-nineteenth century onwards. The other is alive as a daily existential threat, of Western democracies, especially the United States, plotting to undermine and weaken the Party's rule and by extension China itself.

The relationship between China and the United States, as many senior leaders in Beijing recognise, is more complex than the stark notes struck in Chinese propaganda. It is true that the United States, through policies pursued by different arms of the government, intelligence agencies and non-government organisations, has at times striven to undermine Party rule, be it through sending CIA agents into Tibet in the 1950s or seeding pro-democracy groups later on. Beijing saw Washington's hand behind the so-called colour revolutions that upended governments in countries such as Ukraine and Georgia in the early years of this century. The upheaval of the Arab Spring, including the way protesters used social media sites such as Facebook to rouse and organise their supporters, only bolstered their fear of foreign subversion. In the post-Mao era, however, the United States has by and large been, at least until Donald Trump's election, the indispensable enabler of China's rise.

The US military's deployment in East Asia kept the peace in a region riddled with unresolved conflicts involving China, including on the Korean Peninsula and with Taiwan and Japan, allowing Beijing to focus on economic development. When it joined the World Trade Organization (WTO) in 2001, Beijing was able to plug into a global system that it had done nothing to help build. The United States has admitted many of China's brightest young students into its best universities. It helped establish numerous Chinese industries, such as aviation. For long periods, the United States was China's biggest export market. If America was trying to keep China down, as Beijing's persistent propaganda says, it was going about it in a strange way.

When Joe Biden met Xi Jinping in 2011, the then US vice president was hit with a volley of questions from China's leader in waiting about US politics. How did the system work, Xi asked. What was the relationship between the White House and the Congress? How should Beijing interpret the political signals coming out of Washington? For Biden and his advisers, these were all pointed, if predictable, questions, but welcome nonetheless. After nearly a decade of frustration in dealing with the colourless, impenetrable Hu Jintao, the White House had made a deliberate decision to engage Xi a year out from his slated promotion to head the ruling communist party, scheduled for late 2012.

But in lengthy conversations spread over meetings and meals in two cities, Beijing and Chengdu, the capital of Sichuan province, the American visitors were struck by Xi's animation on another topic. Chinese leaders are generally cautious about straying too deeply into biography. Recounting their personal stories in front of their own officials, let alone foreigners, involves traversing recent Chinese political history, a minefield strewn with purges, betrayals and ideological about-turns. Xi, however, talked unprompted about his father, a storied revolutionary from the early days of the Communist Party, and about Mao Zedong, the founder of modern China who had turned the country upside down to keep rivals at bay and stay in power. Once promoted as a loyal retainer, Mao purged Xi's father in 1962 and later jailed him and left him to suffer public humiliation at the hands of the Red Guards in the Cultural Revolution. His father was not rehabilitated until the late 1970s, after Mao had died. Xi himself, as a young man, was harassed by radicals and banished to the countryside during this period. As Xi made clear to his visitors, however, he would not repudiate Mao. Instead, he revered him, along with Deng and his father.

Biden and his advisers left China with an impression of Xi that has turned out to be right – that he would be tougher to deal with than Hu, more ambitious for his country and more assertive about prosecuting what he believed to be China's interests. Even then, they probably underestimated him. In retrospect, it was his personal story that laid down the hard markers for the unyielding leader that Xi would become. For Xi, the centrality of the Party, of Mao, and of his own family, was all of a piece. To deny one part of the CCP's history was to deny the whole corpus. In Xi's eyes, the most important quality for a Chinese leader is to be 'red', which is another way of saying one who is loyal to the Communist Party, its leader and its ideological roots, in good times and bad. Through his revolutionary lineage, lengthy work in the service of the Party and enduring loyalty to its bosses, Xi made his position clear. He would be the reddest leader of all in his generation. Not only that, he expected all party members to follow in his footsteps.

In his conversations with Biden, as with his public record generally, Xi displayed no visceral hostility to the West, as some in the Chinese system do. Certainly, he has made it clear in the past that he doesn't appreciate foreign criticism. 'Some foreigners with full bellies and nothing better to do engage in finger-pointing at us,' Xi complained in a speech in Mexico in 2009 to the Chinese community, and later leaked at a time when he was the heir apparent. 'First, China does not export revolution; second, it does not export famine and poverty; and third, it does not mess around with you. So what else is there to say?'[10]

Xi's focus has not been primarily on the threat from malevolent outside forces, ever present as they may be. His interest has been on building the resilience and capacity to resist and repel them. On coming to office, Xi didn't look with fury at the behaviour of the United States. Rather, he looked with alacrity at the fall of the Soviet Union. Xi was horrified at how the Party had almost evaporated overnight in the Soviet Union. 'A big party was gone just like that,' he said. 'Proportionally, the Soviet Communist Party had more members than [China does], but nobody was man enough to stand up and resist.'[11] China studied intensely the collapse of the Soviet Union in its immediate aftermath. Nearly a quarter of century later, a period during which the Chinese economy had increased twenty-four fold, Xi was worried enough about the state of the Party to make everyone from top leaders to rank-and-file officials go back to class to learn the lessons of the Soviet fall again.[12]

The Soviet collapse has been blamed on many disparate forces, from economic stagnation, corruption and falling oil prices to the draining competition to match Ronald Reagan's arms build-up. But a six-part Chinese documentary about the collapse of the Soviet Union, which at Xi's direction became required viewing for cadres, zeroed in on another factor – the 'infiltration of subversive Western values' and their role in Gorbachev's ultimately unsuccessful economic reforms.[13] Just as Vladimir Putin mourned the fall of the Soviet Union, so too did Xi, for the same reasons that he has always refused to disown Mao Zedong. In Shenzhen, in 2012, Xi made his own views clear. 'To dismiss the history of the Soviet Union and the Soviet Communist Party, to dismiss Lenin and Stalin, and to dismiss everything else is to engage in historic nihilism,' he said in the leaked speech. 'It confuses our thoughts and undermines the party's organisations on all levels.'[14]

The trajectory of Putin's career contained lessons for Xi and the Chinese Communist Party as well. In late 1989, Putin, then a KGB agent in East Germany, phoned Moscow to get instructions when demonstrators gathered outside the local headquarters in Dresden in the tumult that followed the fall of the Berlin Wall. 'Moscow is silent,' Putin was told, in a comment that his biographers say had a profound impact on his world view.[15] The power vacuum that Putin despaired of in Moscow at the time was taken to heart by Xi, who thought China would be vulnerable to the 'hostile foreign forces' only if it let its guard down and allowed the Party to weaken and atrophy. Xi was determined that Beijing would never be silent on his watch.

Xi's anxieties were accentuated by the manoeuvring of two rivals: Bo Xilai, the Chongqing party secretary, and Zhou Yongkang, in charge of internal security. The two Politburo members were detained by the Party after lengthy investigations in 2012 and 2013, respectively, largely on charges of corruption and abuse of power. Their fall amounted to an earthquake in Chinese politics. Bo was a charismatic son of a revolutionary hero making a noisily public run for entry into the leadership's inner circle, the Politburo Standing Committee. Zhou was a member of the standing committee until the end of 2012 and wielded enormous power through his control of the secret police and his sway over the energy sector. Their trials put on display their alleged crimes and amoral womanising. Later, they were accused of political misdeeds that, within the Party, were worse than mere corruption. The official media, quoting senior officials, said the pair had been conspiring to mount an internal coup to seize control of the Party, and effectively to prevent Xi from ascending to the top party post for which he had been groomed.[16]

All this weighed on Xi as he took charge of the Party in late 2012, and spurred him into a frenzy of action. His first 200 days in office stretched across an extraordinary breadth of policy, implemented at an astonishing pace. Within weeks he attached a brand to his administration, the 'China Dream', set strict new rules governing the behaviour of officials, and laid down markers on what ideas could and couldn't be discussed with a crackdown on a liberal newspaper in southern China over its promotion of constitutionalism, a dirty word in a single-party state. Xi also started locking up the Party's critics. Activist lawyers who had carved out a small space to protect citizens' rights were rounded up, one by one, by state security. About 250 lawyers were questioned or detained in a lengthy, methodical campaign, with the last of the prominent human rights lawyers, Wang Quanzhang, not formally sentenced until January 2019 after four years in detention.[17]

Xi's breakneck pace did not let up for the rest of 2013. Within months, Xi had unveiled the Belt and Road Initiative, which gave maximum impetus to Beijing's plan to make China the hub of business and technology all the way to Europe. A new bank to fund infrastructure in the region, the Asian Infrastructure Investment Bank, was set up over US objections. Xi set targets to eradicate poverty by

2021, the 100th anniversary of the founding of the Communist Party in China. In October 2013, he raised the temperature on Taiwan, calling it a political issue that 'cannot be passed on from generation to generation'.[18] Soon after, China set about executing a long-held plan to build large military bases in the South China Sea.

Most important of all, Xi launched his anti-corruption campaign, appointing as its spearhead Wang Qishan, one of the toughest and most capable officials of his generation. To signal their seriousness, Bo Xilai, who had been detained in early 2012, was tried in public early in Xi's first year in office. The Chinese people had not witnessed such a spectacle since Jiang Qing, better known as Madame Mao, was put in the dock with other members of the 'Gang of Four' in 1980. It didn't all go to plan, as the flamboyant Bo used the stage to declare his innocence and label his chief accuser a liar.[19] This state-sanctioned drama was backed up by Xi's issuance of a new set of rules – the Eight-Point Regulations – directing that officials adopt a more austere, close-to-the-grassroots lifestyle.

To wrench China out of the Mao era, Deng Xiaoping had attempted to limit the role of the Party and energise the skills of government. Such distinctions are sometimes dismissed as a mere chimera, as senior government officials have always been, with rare exceptions, party members. But the distinction was an important symbol of the separation of political management from professional policymaking. The visible retreat of the Party and politics drove much of the success of the early reform era in the 1980s, with leaders increasingly shunning old-fashioned central planning in favour of decentralisation and the market.

Xi's administration jettisoned such distinctions, with Wang bluntly announcing in early 2017 that 'there is no such thing as separation between the party and the government. There is only a division of functions.'[20] The change was already evident to anyone paying attention. The State Council, which is China's Cabinet, was the weakest in memory. Li Keqiang, the Premier and notionally China's second-ranked national leader, had ceded, or been forced to cede, numerous key roles to Xi, most notably that of chief economic policymaker. A year later, at the annual National People's Congress in early 2018, the new regime was set in stone, with a host of functions that had long been under government agencies, ranging from management of religion and culture to the oversight and investigation of public sector workers, formally bought under the control of the Party. The move was consistent with the overarching theme of Xi's administration. At every turn, Xi and his cohorts have striven to make the Party paramount.

The contrast with the way Xi took power and Hu Jintao's political inheritance and agenda could not have been starker. When Hu became party secretary in 2002, Beijing had only just entered the WTO, with uncertain prospects. Few Chinese, including the officials who had negotiated the accession deal, knew how successfully China would navigate what lay ahead.[21]

Likewise, China's military power in 2002 was a fraction of what Xi inherited ten years later. Beijing had neither the capability nor confidence to press territorial claims in the South and East China Seas, nor pursue the country's long-term aim of becoming the dominant power in Asia. Deng Xiaoping's old dictum, for China to 'hide its strength and bide its time' on the world stage, was not just a clever formulation. It also artfully matched Beijing's strategic situation.

It has become fashionable to brand the government of Hu and his Premier, Wen Jiabao, as 'ten wasted years'. By many measures, however, Hu and Wen were a huge success. When Xi ascended to the leadership of the Party, China was immeasurably richer, more technologically advanced and more confident about its ability to make its way in the world than it had been a decade earlier. Xi also took charge of a Chinese military that was better equipped and more capable than at any time in the previous two centuries. The days of wondering if China would ever become a world power were gone. The only question was what kind of power China would be.

All of which raises the question of why Xi took office with such anxiety. From today's vantage point, Xi looks like a decisive leader. But taking into account the fevered political atmosphere in 2012 as he took office, Xi's early days seem more like a panicky reaction to threats from powerful enemies than a carefully considered plan to chart a new course for China. At the time, Xi was also reacting with fury to the laxity in the system that had developed under Hu and Wen. Big state enterprises had become vast, ungovernable and often corrupt, and local governments had morphed into borrowing machines that no authority could rein in. Hu was first among equals in the Politburo. To rule on his own terms, Xi had to make sure he had no challengers in the senior leadership.

There has been much hand-wringing in the West about how so many experts got China, and Xi, so wrong. But it is not clear whether Xi's colleagues knew what they were getting when they tapped him in 2007 to be Hu's successor either. Xi, after all, had emerged as the compromise candidate at that year's party congress. Certainly, he was a seasoned official from impeccable CCP lineage, and acceptable to both dominant groupings at the top – the 'Shanghai Gang' and its titular head, Jiang Zemin, and the clique clustered around the China Youth League, headed by Hu. According to one report, party elders settled on Xi because he was pliable and 'lacked a power base'.[22] At most, Xi seems to have been given the nod to re-centralise authority in Beijing after a decade in which power had been dispersed through the far-flung system in multiple fiefdoms. If that was Xi's mandate from the party elders, he has gone far beyond it in office.

Xi has been called China's new emperor, a title that he now commands with ease. In contrast, Hu was a timid figure in internal politics, an emperor in name only, crippled by the rival princes and conspiring courtiers who surrounded him from the outset. But applying the moniker of emperor to Xi can be misleading, as it conjures up an image of a stately imperial figure presiding with traditional benevolence and little attention to detail over a vast state and citizenry. Xi has been anything but above the fray in office. He is more akin to one of those swordsmen in a popular martial arts movie, daring multiple opponents to take him on, and then slaying them in a series of bloody showdowns. Xi is never bracketed with his Premier, Li Keqiang, in describing his administration, as Hu was with Wen. More than any Chinese leader since Mao, Xi has set the tone himself.

Along the way, the casualties have piled up.

CHAPTER TWO

The law is strong

In October 2018, China's official press curtly reported that Zhang Yang, one of the country's most senior generals, had been expelled from the Party and the military. In some respects, there was nothing unusual about the announcement, as it simply amounted to official confirmation that Zhang had been under investigation for corruption. Just as the Party has its own military, it runs an in-house anti-corruption and detention system, the Central Commission for Discipline Inspection. The Party delivers its verdicts on the guilt or innocence of officials who are put under investigation, although not in robes from the bench in a public court. The Party has its own way of conveying guilt, through the act of expulsion from its ranks. The legal system only kicks in later, after the Party has ruled on the guilt of the official under investigation.

To the public, Zhang had been a colourless apparatchik, a stern figure usually pictured loyally in the presence of Xi Jinping and the Politburo, distinguished by his military uniform, moonish features and a tight, jet-black comb-over that covered his head like a wig. Within the system, however, he was a powerful player. Zhang had been in charge of the Political Work Department in the People's Liberation Army (PLA). That title alone tells you a lot about China. As Xi often reminds the military, the PLA is not the country's army. It is the military arm of the ruling Communist Party, and has been since its foundation in 1927. Even as the PLA has developed into a professional, high-tech fighting force, senior officers such as Zhang had the job of ghosting commanders at the same rank, to make sure they stayed loyal to the Party. In retrospect, it was clear that the authorities should have been keeping a closer eye on Zhang himself.

There was one element that made Zhang's case stand out, however. By the time he was expelled from the Party, Zhang had been dead for nearly a year. In November 2017, Zhang was found hung from the ceiling at his mansion in Guangzhou, across the border from Hong Kong. The first sign that his suicide was related to corruption came in the press coverage of his death. Despite his decades of service and seniority, Zhang received anything but a respectful send-off. After his body was found, the PLA's official newspaper called the late general a man 'with no moral bottom line' and said his death was a 'shameful way to end his life' and a 'bad move to escape punishment'.[23]

Zhang is not the first party member to be posthumously expelled. In the clean-up after the chaos and brutality of Mao Zedong's reign, Kang Sheng, the CCP's secret police chief for periods both before and after the Cultural Revolution, was expelled from the Party five years after his death, in 1980, for his role in the excesses of the revolution. When the political winds started to blow in the opposite direction in the Deng era, another of Mao's henchmen suffered the same indignity. Xie Fuzhi, a rough and tough security official who armed Red Guards to fight Mao's enemies, was not only expelled from the Party after his death. His ashes were dug up, removed from the Babaoshan Revolutionary Cemetery in west Beijing and tossed to the winds. The Party has always been unsentimental about those who fall from grace.

Zhang's case, and the fate of other senior figures toppled in the anti-corruption scandal, was telling nonetheless. The numbers of officials locked up by

Xi has been staggering. Since late 2012, the authorities have investigated more than 2.7 million officials and punished more than 1.5 million others. They include seven at the top level (that is, at the level of the Politburo and the Cabinet), and about two-dozen high-ranking generals. Two senior officials have been sentenced to death.[24] In a party with more than 80 million members, once you exclude the tens of millions who are farmers, elderly and retired, all largely spared in the campaign, that amounts to a generational clean-out. Zhang's posthumous expulsion was just another reminder that in Xi's China, even death is no saviour. For serious offenders, the Party will hunt you and your family down beyond the grave.

Senior Chinese leaders of all stripes have long talked a big game on anti-corruption. Until Xi, however, no one had followed through. His anti-corruption campaign was audacious and risky on many levels. Xi didn't just take down millions of local officials who, until the moment they were detained, lived lives of power and privilege and in many cases enjoyed wealth wildly out of step with their official salaries. He took on hundreds of senior officials in the elite nomenklatura as well. All of these officials, from the top to the bottom of the system, were in effect power centres in their own right – in the capital, provinces, cities and villages, and in state industries and private corporate empires. Each official anchored the wealth of multiple families and loyalists. In other words, in cracking down on corruption, Xi might have won popular support but he also earned himself a bucketload of bitter enemies, all itching for revenge.

Superficially, Xi's campaign had little in common with the other great upheavals of Chinese politics since 1949. But the Anti-Rightist Movement, the Great Leap Forward, the Cultural Revolution and the mass purge that followed the 1989 military suppression of pro-democracy demonstrators were all in one way or another a product of similar phenomenon to Xi's crackdown, of top-level power struggles that resulted in individual leaders deciding they needed to shake up the Party. The campaigns all left scars in the system, which decades later still linger, largely unresolved. There is no reason to think the impact of Xi's campaign will be any different.

In the decade before Xi came to power, corruption in China worked almost like a transaction tax that greased the wheels of commerce and business. Many senior officials turned a blind eye to the problem, either because they were corrupt themselves, or because they saw the kickbacks as a way to spread the system's benefits and give poorly paid officials a greater stake in the government. 'For who else can the regime depend upon for support but the great masses of middle-level cadres?' says the narrator in the mid-1990s book *The Wrath of Heaven*, a sensational roman à clef about the then Beijing mayor. 'If they are not given some advantages, why should they dedicate themselves to the regime?' Corruption, the book's narrator concludes, 'makes our political system more stable'.[25]

By the time Xi arrived, corruption, far from making the system more stable, was threatening to hollow out the Chinese state as it had done in Suharto's Indonesia and numerous African nations. Failing to fight graft, Xi said, could lead to 'the collapse of the Party and the downfall of the state'.[26] Legal scholars had long complained about the system's extra-judicial powers, according to which officials can be detained for months and subject to endless interrogations without access to a lawyer. But Xi had little tolerance for such complaints. On the contrary, the executive power wielded by the anti-corruption commission offered just the weapon Xi needed to get his way. The Party newspapers described the system's fearsome qualities with approval, as a kind of net that covered the sky, 'an eye that can see thousands of miles and an ear that hears everything the wind blows its way'.[27]

Controversial long before Xi came to power, the Central Commission for Discipline Inspection sits above the courts, the police and the law. That is why, when officials are toppled, the wrongdoings listed in the official media often include offences that are not crimes of themselves, such as leading a debauched lifestyle and taking on mistresses. 'Party discipline', as the collection of rules governing cadres' behaviour is called, is stricter than the law, and officials are in theory held to higher standards than mere members of the public.

For Xi and his advisers, the anti-corruption campaign had multiple uses. It acted as a kind of magic weapon that, all at once, could stop the cancer of graft from spreading and hollowing out the bureaucracy and the military, as well as keeping cadres loyal to Xi and helping manage the economy. Other leaders might have failed to use the body's powers. An anxious Xi was not about to make that mistake himself. Not only did he make full use of the existing system, he extended it.

In early 2018, the National People's Congress created a new super agency, the National Supervision Commission, which took in the operations of the party's anti-graft body. The same powers that the Party's anti-corruption body employed to manage senior Party members were now to be applied to all civil servants, whether they were senior CCP members or not. As outlined by Wang Qishan, the Party needed to tighten control over all aspects of public life, which meant strengthening supervision over 'all public servants who exercise public power'.[28] In other words, the commission's fearsome extra-judicial powers would effectively become the legal standard for large swathes of the working bureaucracy.

As a politically supervised body, the commission has naturally always been open to political manipulation. Jiang Zemin, for example, had the Beijing Mayor, Chen Xitong, a political rival, arrested for corruption in 1995. Likewise, Hu Jintao's biggest scalp in his decade in office was the Shanghai Party Secretary, Chen Liangyu, who had defied the Beijing leadership over economic policy and who was dismissed in 2006. In both cases, the two Chens (no relation) were easily pinned for corruption, expelled from the Party, tried and convicted in the courts, and then jailed. But their crimes were as much due to losing internal power struggles with the central government as breaking any law.

Xi and Wang had specific targets in their campaign: the top rungs of the military, the oil industry (or the 'petroleum gang', as the power clique is known) and the finance sector, along with some provinces, especially Shaanxi, a coal industry hub. Some sectors were targeted because of their association with big fish such as Zhou Yongkang, who, before he took over as China's state security tsar, held sway atop the energy sector. Others were caught up as investigators probed vulnerable cadres and followed the family and cash that trailed behind them.

A number of the targets appeared blatantly political. Sun Zhengcai, party secretary of the city-province of Chongqing, was abruptly removed from office in July 2017. It was just months ahead of the Communist Party and National People's Congresses, which would both confirm Xi for a second term in office and dispense with any time limits on him ever stepping down. Before he was toppled, Sun was considered a potential rival to Xi. In an instant, he was gone. The following year, in 2018, Sun was sentenced to life imprisonment. By and large, it is hard to make the case that the prime purpose of Xi's anti-corruption campaign was to remove his political enemies. But Sun's detention was a reminder that, when necessary, rivals could be targeted as well. It also reinforced a lesson that most officials had already absorbed, that Xi would not allow any competition at the top of the Party.

In the military, for example, the anti-corruption campaign was aligned with Xi's larger aim, to make senior party members 'red and professional' (politically reliable and competent) and clean, or at least cleaner. Two of the senior generals removed, Xu Caihou and Zhang Yang, were reported, among other things, to have been selling commissions. The problem of senior military officers and government officials selling promotions to underlings has long been acknowledged as corrosive to the notion of meritocracy that the Party prides itself on, let alone military capabilities. It is not hard to see how Xi, who was investing billions of dollars in readying the military to take on all comers, would be horrified at the idea that Chinese soldiers were being commanded by people who had bought their promotions.

The anti-corruption campaign was also a tool of economic management. The boom spawned by the huge stimulus that Beijing engineered to lift the economy out of its slump during the global financial crisis in 2008 had a number of effects beyond resuscitating output. Local officials became addicted to big-spending infrastructure projects, which helped them meet growth targets and allowed them and their cronies to pocket huge windfall profits along the way. But they also left a mountain of debt that the state, in one form or another, would have to clean up. In recent years, Beijing's technocrats have tried to push policies that encourage consumption and pull the economy off the old mainstays of investment and infrastructure. China wants to cut debt, not create more. In that respect, the anti-corruption campaign was a lever of fiscal policy as well. If local officials felt able to ignore central diktats in the Hu Jintao era, they were much more circumspect with Xi's anti-corruption brigade breathing down their necks.

Xi and Wang vowed to go after both 'tigers and flies', which is to say officials of all ranks, no matter how big or small. The phrase 'tigers and flies', heavily publicised by the Chinese media at the outset of the anti-graft crackdown in January 2013, has its origins in a campaign against financial corruption in Shanghai in 1948, a year before the founding of the People's Republic of China. The so-called 'tiger-beating teams' under the then Nationalist/ Kuomintang leader Chiang Kai-shek targeted speculators and hoarders, including the criminal gangs that held sway over the port city. The name came from their chant: 'We beat tigers; we do not swat flies.' Xi and Wang, however, targeted both categories.

To get a sense of the magnitude of the clean-out since Xi came to power in late 2012 and its dual systemic and personal impact, try to imagine a similar, sweeping anti-corruption campaign in the United States. Such an exercise requires an intellectual leap, as the United States does not have a unitary anti-graft body that can simultaneously investigate government officials, military officers, business executives, state governors, financial regulators, the police and intelligence agencies, city mayors and think tank scholars.

The nearest equivalent might be someone like special counsel Robert Mueller, whose brief was to examine allegations of collusion with Russia during Donald Trump's 2016 election campaign. But the Chinese system is much more than that. It is like having a standing corps of special prosecutors spread throughout the system, at all levels of government and within state companies, without any of the guardrails that restrain the likes of Mueller. US investigators have great power but they must follow the law and eventually have their allegations tested in courts. None of those strictures apply in China. The other big difference, of course, is that whereas Mueller was empowered to investigate the president, China's anti-graft squads went nowhere near Xi.[29]

Outwardly, Xi as a leader is a figure of rectitude, with no known vices apart from once being a smoker. He has also reportedly issued the standard warnings that Chinese leaders deliver about ensuring their families don't benefit from their power. 'Rein in your spouses, children, relatives, friends and staff, and vow not to use power for personal gain,' he told officials during a 2004 conference call, according to one report.[30] It was advice that Xi's own family clearly did not heed.

In June 2012, Bloomberg published an extensively documented account of the wealth accumulated by Xi's close relatives, notably his sister and brother-in-law.[31] In 2014, *The New York Times* published a report related to the same topic, this time detailing how Xi's family had begun unloading hundreds of millions of dollars of their investments.[32] This remarkable story was anchored by an on-the-record confirmation from a Hong Kong-based Chinese financier, Xiao Jianhua, who had bought some of the assets. He said Xi's sister and her husband were selling their stakes 'for the family'. Xiao knew a great deal about senior Chinese leaders' financial affairs, maybe too much. In January 2017, Xiao was abducted from his apartment at the Four Seasons, overlooking Hong Kong harbour, and transported back to China. He has not been heard from since.

Members of Xi's family, however, have never been detained by the authorities. Neither have Wen

Jiabao's family. Wen's family wealth was detailed in an earlier *New York Times* report, in late 2012.[33] His wife and son had long been the subject of complaints about their business dealings, including during Wen's ten years in power as Premier under Hu Jintao. In the early years of the Xi administration, rumours circulated that members of the Wen family were under investigation, but no action was ever taken against them. In retrospect, the speculation looked like a ploy to keep Wen in a box, an unsubtle reminder that if the former Premier spoke up against Xi or opposed his policies, he and his family could be taken down for their business dealings.[34]

The number of 'tigers' toppled by Xi's campaign – officials who were once part of the designated elite and whose jobs had to be cleared through the Party's central personnel system – is difficult to calculate. The best estimates put it at around 300 to 400, including scores of generals. The officials who have lost their jobs and, in many cases, have been prosecuted and jailed, include members of the Politburo, ministers, vice-ministers, the heads of state-owned enterprises who have ministerial status in the system, provincial party leaders and governors, and city leaders and mayors. With rare exceptions, once the Party puts an official or military officer under investigation, their career is over.

To get a full measure of the anti-corruption campaign and why it will be felt in Chinese politics for
years to come, it is important to count not just the
400-odd senior officials, state business executives
and military officers felled directly. In each of those
cases, the investigation doesn't just hit the individual
official who has been targeted and detained. Literally
hundreds of people who are tied into and rely on
that single person for their livelihood are effectively
swept up with them. The elite patronage networks
include direct and distant family members, and clus-
ters of people working alongside and under them in
state companies, in party and government offices,
in ministries and the military. In many cases, it also
includes the scores of people who profit from the
official's financial dealings through the investment
vehicles that are spun out of and sustained by their
ill-gotten wealth. Pull down one person and you
destroy hundreds if not thousands of people along
with them. Their livelihoods, and all that they have
invested in clawing their way through the system,
can evaporate with the stroke of a pen. Some members of the patronage networks are often arrested
themselves.

Hundreds of thousands of powerful and privileged
members of China's elite have had their careers, status, and in many cases their wealth, taken from them

almost overnight. Xi has made enemies of them all. 'Xi has destroyed millions of people in the elite who now all hold a personal grudge against him,' said a China-based businessman, who asked not to be named. 'These people are not a bunch of uneducated peasants from the sticks in Henan. They had skin in the game.'[35]

The seniority of the toppled officials is not the sole measure of the campaign's impact. As Andrew Wedeman of Georgia State University, an expert on the Chinese corruption system, points out, the amounts of money stolen at a local level are often just as significant. On top of the big shots, that is the 'tigers' pulled down by the central anti-corruption authorities, scholars added two more categories: the 'rats' (at the country level) and the 'wolves' (at the prefecture level), both of which 'have raked in huge sums and gotten away with it for years', according to Wedeman.[36] These local officials, too, have had their wealth and power taken from them, as have the people in their networks who lived off them. So while Xi may have cleansed the Party of many corrupt officials, he created for himself a multitude of foes, spread throughout the system.

In its initial stages, the intensity of the anti-corruption campaign was often explained away by Xi supporters. They described it as something of a one-off house-cleaning exercise that, once completed, would lay the ground for further reforms advancing the rule of law. This explanation was in line with many early views of Xi, that he was, in Chinese political terms, 'turning left so that he could turn right'. In other words, he was shoring up the conservative base of the Party, the 'left' in China, before shifting to the 'right', or pushing for more market-based, liberal reforms.

In fact, Xi did the opposite. With the establishment of the new National Supervision Commission in 2018, he extended the extra-judicial reach of the Party with the result that he also alienated large slabs of the legal intelligentsia. His decision infuriated the country's scholars who had worked valiantly for years, not always with success, to advance the rule of law and build an independent court system. In August 2017, a group of 59 Chinese lawyers and legal scholars issued a joint letter to the National People's Congress saying the rule of law 'faced a crisis'. Anyone under investigation who had rights under the criminal law, they said, would find those same rights extinguished under the new supervision commission. 'Is such logic (not) ridiculous?' they wrote, adding that the misuse of power was inevitable.[37] A more pithy critique was delivered by a well-known dissident, Gao Hongming. 'Under the absolute leadership of the Party,' Gao wrote, 'the people are nothing; the state is nothing; the constitution is nothing; the law is nothing. The Chinese judicial system is [the] Communist Party.'[38]

Such complaints had little impact. With Xi bearing down upon them, the priority for officials was not to question Xi's leadership but to implement his policy. In 2017, when the new rules were being gradually rolled out in select areas, provinces began competing to implement Xi's edict. In Zhejiang, a wealthy coastal province, the leaders of the local anti-corruption commission announced that their remit now extended to more than 700 000 civil servants, an increase of 83 per cent.[39] In Hainan, the number of people subject to the new strictures jumped more than tenfold. Some scholars defended the new commission, depicting it as the inevitable product of the Party absorbing the state. Deng had been 'misunderstood' on the need to separate the Party and state, said one scholar. 'We should insist on the Party's core leadership in co-ordinating everything,' said Zhang Rongcheng, of the Central Party School.[40]

Xi himself quoted one of China's most famous philosophers, Han Fei, the patron saint of the 'legalist' school of philosophy over two millennia ago. 'When those who uphold the law are strong, the law is strong; when those who uphold the law are weak, the law is weak.'[41] Put another way, the ruler sits above the law and commands it as an instrument of power. For Xi, it was the essence of legal reform. For many under him, it was the very opposite of the kind of progress they had pushed for the legal system.

CHAPTER THREE

When in Rome . . .

In September 2018, a Chinese banker in Beijing set the local internet alight with a surprising suggestion: to phase out local entrepreneurs and allow state companies to take their place. 'China's private sector has already done its job in aiding the development of the state economy, and it should now leave the stage,' wrote Wu Xiaoping in a blog post.[42] Wu's big idea was as simple as it was outlandish. In readiness for a showdown with the United States and other hostile foreign powers, China had to consolidate its economic gains under a single, unified state banner. The blind development of the private sector, he argued, should give way to a strengthened state economy and large enterprises under the Party's control. Wu's post was roundly attacked and ridiculed. Even the *People's Daily*, the Communist Party's official mouthpiece, weighed in to run it down. The bigger question, though, given the heavyweight criticism of the post, was why Wu's ramblings hit such a nerve in the first place.

The days of anyone disputing the central role of the private sector in sustaining the Chinese economy are long gone. The Chinese use a single figure – '56789' – to describe how the private sector supports the economy. Entrepreneurs contribute 50 per cent of tax revenue, 60 per cent of output, 70 per cent of industrial modernisation and innovation, 80 per cent of jobs, and 90 per cent of enterprises. Although not entirely accurate, the figure symbolically encapsulates the core truth of modern China and the Communist Party – that the country's economy and political system would have run aground long ago without the country's entrepreneurs.

Wu's blog post ignited criticism partly because of his employer, the country's biggest local investment bank, although his co-workers at China International Capital Corporation dismissed him as something of a professional stirrer. But the real explanation for the backlash firestorm was his timing. Wu's article landed in dry tinder, amid rising anxiety among entrepreneurs who were being deprived of capital, hurt by a slowing economy and buffeted by Donald Trump's tariffs. They were all important factors in the gloom that was settling over private business at the time. The root of the entrepreneurs' concern, however, was elsewhere. It was political, in the form of Xi Jinping.

By 2012, the year Xi came to power, private firms were responsible for about half of all investment in China and the bulk of GDP. Nicholas Lardy, a US economist with a long track record of studying the Chinese economy, said that Xi's ascension marked a turning point for entrepreneurs. 'Since 2012,' he wrote in a book released in early 2019, 'this picture of private, market-driven growth has given way to a resurgence of the role of the state in resource allocation and a shrinking role for the market and private firms.'[43]

China watchers differ about the degree to which Xi's leadership marks a clear break in economic policymaking. Chinese state firms have always had a predominant role in the economy, long before Xi took over the country's leadership. In the political pecking order of the economy, the state always sits at the top.[44] Equally, the Party has always maintained direct control over state firms through the power to hire and fire senior executives, along with other levers. For more than a decade, the Party has tried to ensure it played a role inside private businesses as well. Both central and local governments have long offered a variety of subsidies for both public and private firms, especially to bolster indigenous technology.

Still, however one characterises past policies, there is little doubt that Xi firmly positioned himself on the side of party intervention and state control. In his first term, Xi spoke constantly of the need to support the state economy rather than abandon it. The Party's role in both government and private businesses was solidified and expanded. The number of industrial funds run by the government and those doling out public money soared. The central government stepped in with billions of dollars in support when the stock market threatened to melt down in 2015. Local governments took their cue from the centre, offering loans to prop up so-called 'zombie companies', government-owned enterprises that would otherwise have gone bankrupt. As one astute commentator on Lardy's book noted, the general explanation for Xi's policy stance, that he didn't understand the benefits of free markets, was wrong. In fact, the opposite might be true: that Xi understands markets more than well enough to know the threat they pose to single-party rule.[45]

Xi's interventionist instincts have had profound ramifications in China and abroad, and solidified his critics' narrative about him in other areas. For example, when US officials were pressed in early 2019 to provide evidence that Huawei, the Chinese telecommunications giant, had facilitated spying on the United States and its allies, they said there was no need. Beijing had already made their case for them, first with the Party's systematic infiltration of private companies, and second with the passage of a new national intelligence law in 2017. The law states that 'any organisation and citizen' shall support and cooperate 'in national intelligence work'.[46] The director of America's National Counterintelligence and Security Center, when asked about China's entrepreneurs, cited these two policies in asserting that 'Chinese company relationships with the Chinese government aren't like private sector company relationships with governments in the West'.[47]

From such conclusions, important policy changes flow. The United States and European Union were immediately gifted an excuse to limit Chinese access to their markets, technology and companies. Australia has cited the same intelligence law to keep Huawei's 5G technology out of its future mobile networks. Gordon Sondland, Donald Trump's envoy to the European Union, gave such sentiment a hyperbolic spin to argue that Europe should do the same. 'We want to keep critical infrastructure in the Western world out of Chinese malign influence,'

Sondland said. 'Someone from the Politburo in Beijing picks up the phone and says "I wanna listen in on the following conversation, I wanna run a certain car off the road that's on the 5G network and kill the person that's in it," there's nothing that company legally can do today in China to prevent the Chinese government from making that request successfully.'[48]

Until recently, such a statement would have been laughed out of court. No longer. Nor would Washington have contemplated the policy of 'decoupling' the US and Chinese economies, shorthand for the administration's commitment, through taxes, tariffs and other punitive measures, to disentangle its companies and their technologies from China's supply chains. As Henry Paulson, the former Goldman Sachs chief, erstwhile US treasury secretary and long-time China bull, said in a speech in November 2018: 'I see more clearly than ever the prospect of an economic Iron Curtain – one that throws up new walls on each side and unmakes the global economy, as we have known it.'[49]

Within China, the backlash against Xi's economic policies has been framed differently. Few critics of government policy take Xi head on. Rather, they place the debate on safer ground by focusing on the success of decades of reform. Numerous high-profile scholars used the 40th anniversary of economic reform to warn against the reinforcement of the state model. Wu Jinglian, 89, a pioneering market economist, said increasing state command of the economy would lead to 'crony capitalism' and revive memories of the 1950s, when the Party forced private companies to hand over their assets.[50] Zhang Weiying, of Peking University, another prominent market economist, said Beijing was flattering itself if it believed it had developed according to a unique model of economics rather than getting wealthy through the market like other countries. 'The theory of the "China model" sets China as a frightening anomaly from the Western perspective,' he said, 'and inevitably leads to confrontation between China and the West.'[51] In May 2019, the outgoing head of the national pension fund and former finance minister, Lou Jiwei, called the state funding of local technology projects a 'waste of taxpayers' money'.[52]

The sharpest attack on Xi's economic policies was delivered towards the end of 2018. In a speech initially posted on the internet before being taken down, Professor Xiang Songzuo of Renmin University said: 'Since the beginning of the year . . . all kinds of ideological statements have been thrown around: statements like "private property will be eliminated", "private ownership will eventually be abolished if not now", "it's time for the private enterprises to fade away", or "all private companies should be turned over to their workers". Then there was this high-profile study of Marx and the Communist Manifesto. Remember that line in the Communist Manifesto? Abolition of private property. What kind of signal do you think this sends to private entrepreneurs?'[53]

The relationship between the Party and private sector companies is, up to a point, flexible and fluid, certainly more so than with state companies. The Party doesn't habitually micromanage their day-to-day operations. The firms are largely still in charge of their basic business decisions. But pressure from party committees to have a seat at the table when executives are making big calls on investment and the like means the 'lines have been dangerously blurred', in the words of one analyst. 'Chinese domestic laws and administrative guidelines, as well as unspoken regulations and internal party committees, make it quite difficult to distinguish between what is private and what is state-owned.'[54] The answer to the question 'does the Party control a company?' is that it is impossible to tell. In the current environment, however, fewer foreign governments want to give Beijing the benefit of the doubt. If there was any question as to who was in charge of the economy and business, Xi's local and overseas critics alike only had to take the Chinese leader at his word, that in private enterprises, as with state-owned firms and every institution in China, the Party was the ultimate authority.

If any Chinese leader appreciated the value of business, it should have been Xi. From 1985 to 2007, Xi served in two provinces, Fujian and Zhejiang, becoming the governor of the former and party secretary of the latter. Both provinces stand out in China as thriving bastions of private enterprise. Fujian was also the premier gateway for investors from nearby Taiwan, starting in the 1980s and accelerating after WTO accession. Like leaders of Fujian before and after him, Xi regularly hosted Taiwanese entrepreneurs and lobbied them to put money into the province. Zhejiang is home to a number of China's most famous and successful private companies, such as Jack Ma's Alibaba in Hangzhou and Li Shufu's Geely, the car manufacturer that bought Sweden's Volvo, in Ningbo.

In the early optimistic glow of Xi's ascension to the leadership, the Western media naturally latched onto his provincial pedigree to talk up his appreciation of markets. Zhejiang's capitalist spirit had rubbed off on Xi, Bloomberg reported, quoting Lu Guanqiu, a businessman who owned and ran Wanxiang, the private car parts group. 'When Xi becomes general secretary, he'll be even more open and will pay even more attention to private enterprise and the people's livelihood,' Lu said. 'It's because he was in Zhejiang for five years.'[55] The arc of Xi's father's career, from revolutionary to reformer, reinforced this optimism.

Yet a deeper dig into Xi's past statements and writings on the economy displays an official who has been a dogged and diligent supporter of party orthodoxy on the economy at every turn. Xi might have taken big risks in domestic and foreign policy but on the economy, he was not one for ideological experimentation. In the Politburo, as vice president from 2008 to 2013 and as the leader of the party school for most of the same period, there is little evidence of him straying from his core beliefs about the need to consolidate and strengthen party control inside businesses. Xi has always talked about development being balanced between the state and the entrepreneurial economy. In practice, though, that meant protecting the state sector to ensure it wasn't eaten up by entrepreneurs in places such as Fujian and Zhejiang.

By the time Xi arrived in Zhejiang in 2002, the province was already well on the way up the economic ladder. Xi, who used to write an occasional newspaper column, headed a group of officials who became known as the 'New Zhijiang Army'. They embraced the use of 'social capital', a euphemism for private investment, to spread the risk in funding the province's signature infrastructure projects, such as the 36-kilometre Hangzhou Bay Bridge connecting Shanghai and Ningbo. Relying solely on government investment is not enough, Xi wrote. 'It is better to walk with two legs than one.'

In 2007, in a conversation with Washington's then Ambassador to Beijing, Clark Randt Jr, recorded in US diplomatic cables and later disseminated by WikiLeaks, Xi delivered a sophisticated, self-aware exposition on Zhejiang. He promoted the province's success over its rival and neighbour, Jiangsu, and other places in China, which was also a way of burnishing his own stewardship of the locality. He didn't pretend that there was any secret to the province's wealth other than local entrepreneurs, although he avoided using the language of the market in describing them. 'Zhejiang has maintained these remarkable results because it is an economy of the grassroots,' Xi said. 'The common people choose their own development paths.'[56]

Xi did what every other official with responsibility for the economy did at the time: he simplified registration for private companies and helped them to access finance. When the Party debated a law to protect private property, he supported it because it helped Zhejiang and, ultimately, China. 'Private property plays a leading role in Zhejiang's economic development, so nearly everyone in Zhejiang agrees with [the] passage of the property law,' Xi told Randt. 'With property protection in place, Chinese can gain even more wealth.'[57] But Xi's support for mixing the duelling ownership structures was purely pragmatic. It had value, he said in another forum, because it would 'improve the socialist market economic structure'.[58] Xi's assessment is echoed by Michael Collins, Deputy Assistant Director of CIA for the East Asia and Pacific Mission Center and one of the Agency's most senior officials for Asia, who said that in China economic reform is not an end to be achieved itself. 'The fundamental end of the Communist Party of China under Xi Jinping is all the more to control that society politically and economically. The economy is being viewed, affected and controlled to achieve a political end.'[59]

By 2012, when Xi came to power, the landscape had changed substantially. China was initially knocked sideways by the global financial crisis in 2008, before swiftly navigating its way back to fast growth through a giant fiscal stimulus orchestrated by the government and delivered by the big state banks. In the same year, China hosted the Olympics, with Xi overseeing Beijing's management of the event. For the Party, China's economic recovery and the Olympics were judged to be triumphs and, as such, affirmations of the governing system's superior qualities and China's enhanced global status.

The economy was also changing shape in this period. From around 2010, after the fiscal splurge of the financial crisis, Chinese technocrats began to focus more intently on cutting debt and lifting consumption. That meant less focus on investment and exports and, if you listened to the entrepreneurs, a greater reliance on private business to generate growth. 'Chinese consumption is not driven by the government but by entrepreneurship, and the market,' Jack Ma of Alibaba said in September 2015. 'In the past 20 years, the government was so strong. Now, they are getting weak. It's our opportunity; it's our show time, to see how the market economy, entrepreneurship, can develop real consumption.'[60] Ma may have thought that the times suited him, and to a degree, they did. His business continued to soar. But Xi was all the time making sure that the Party grew in tandem with the economy, in both the state and private sectors. In retrospect, Ma's comments look dangerously cocky.

The Party has been a constant presence in state-owned firms from their founding after the 1949 revolution. Under Xi, the Party's role has been recalibrated and expanded. As in other areas of policy, Xi was seen as restoring central control after the laxity of the Hu years, a period during which many of the large state enterprises, big enough to be in the top 20 of the global Fortune 500, grew into powerful empires and breeding grounds for serious corruption. In the words of one analyst, Xi 'faced the aftermath of a decade of rapid expansion and weak internal discipline in the state sector'.[61]

In his first term, Xi began reining in the big state firms. In 2015, centrally owned state enterprises were directed to make the Party the 'political core' in running their companies. A year later, Xi chaired a national meeting that cleared the way for a more expansive role for the Party in enterprises, beyond managing staff and keeping an eye on politics. In 2017, the measures were further extended, with the body overseeing big state companies directing them to write the Party into their articles of association. In 2018, the securities regulator followed up by issuing a new corporate governance code requiring listed firms, at home and abroad, to include in their internal guidelines an expansive role for the Party. Many Chinese companies listed in Hong

Kong also wrote the Party's role into their articles of association.[62]

In some ways, codifying in public documents the Party's role in the management of companies was both an instance of rare transparency and part of an increasing trend of the Party openly displaying its power. Chinese state-owned listed companies had customarily filed misleading prospectuses ahead of their stock exchange listings that omitted the Party's pivotal role, including the hiring and firing of senior executives. Similarly, company boards had long been legally and theoretically independent of the Party, but not in practice. 'The same individual who is chairing a Party committee meeting on a Monday might well be chairing a board meeting later in the week,' notes a 2018 report on Chinese corporate governance.[63]

There has always been an awkward fit between Western notions of corporate governance and the party state's insistence on having a role in companies. 'It is rather like drawing a tiger with a cat as a model,' said one Chinese commentator.[64] But the direction of policy under Xi has been clear: the power that the Party had over business decisions and personnel in state firms, once wielded behind the scenes, would not only be strengthened. The Party's power would also increasingly be exercised explicitly, with a demand that it be recognised and acknowledged. With the anti-corruption campaign simultaneously running at full speed, Xi's diktats packed the kind of punch that Hu Jintao's never could.

Sit in meetings with Chinese officials often enough and their talking points become familiar. Some have long been part of the political furniture, ranging from how the Party has lifted 700 million Chinese out of poverty to the existential imperative of re-uniting Taiwan with China. In recent years, in an effort to defend their big state companies, officials have added a new talking point in meetings with foreigners, the concept of 'competitive neutrality'. The phrase embodies the idea that any form of business ownership, be it state or private, can be fair, as long as the policies that govern them are transparent. In the words of the top official overseeing big state companies, Chinese state firms were 'independent market players' responsible for their own operations and profitability and no different from enterprises with 'other forms of ownership'.[65]

So far, however, Chinese protestations about 'competitive neutrality' have fallen on deaf ears. In fact, foreign attitudes against Chinese state companies have hardened. Western nations are setting a higher bar for Chinese state firms to buy their companies. In the case of US technology companies, they are barred altogether. In trade deals such as the Trans-Pacific Partnership, state-owned firms are getting greater scrutiny than private players. In 2017, the United States and European Union both declined to recognise China as a market economy, a status which would have helped Chinese firms fend off claims that its companies were selling goods overseas at below market prices. The United States and European Union had promised to award the market economy label to China in 2016, 15 years after Beijing's accession to the WTO. But they backtracked, citing China's failure to curb the state's role in the economy and the damage to overseas competitors.[66] Worse awaits Beijing, as Xi's shadow now hangs over private firms as well.

Private companies are sometimes written about as if they are a new frontier for the Party, but that is only half true. As early as the turn of the century, around the time Jiang Zemin secured support for allowing entrepreneurs to join the CCP, the Party began to do the same in reverse. If private businesses were coming into the Party, the Party always made sure it had a seat at the table in the companies as well. But under Xi, the same mindset of consolidation and expansion on display within the state sector was also evident within private companies, both local and foreign. In March 2012, a few months before taking over as general secretary, Xi delivered a speech in which he stressed the need to lift both the number of party bodies inside private business, euphemistically known as 'non-publicly owned enterprises', and increase the sorts of work they supervised.[67] Around the same time, new details for 'party building' in enterprises were released, calling 'for the party secretary to participate in and attend important executive-level meetings'.[68]

Many of the regulations issued in 2012 sounded as much like ritualistic incantations of standard propaganda as they do clear directives. They called for 'uniting the masses', 'building an advanced corporate culture' and disseminating the Party's policies and principles. Some reports discussed how the role of the Party was to boost the firms' profits. In Kunshan, in Jiangsu province, near Shanghai, long a hub for Taiwanese investors, officials held a national training class for party secretaries of private companies at which they described the internal committees as the 'nerve endings of the CCP'.[69]

The point about profitability is important, though, as is the injunction to attend 'executive-level meetings'. The Party wants to be part of business successes, not failures. It wants to sit alongside local and foreign entrepreneurs and share their wealth, not run their companies into the ground with socialist dictates. Increasingly, it also wants to do more than supervise companies. It wants to be at the table when commercial decisions are made, not just manage staff. 'We should make money together,' Lu Wei, then head of China's party office for Internet Security, told Paul Jacobs, the CEO of Qualcomm, the US chip maker, in 2014.[70] Lu's comments to some extent reflected Beijing's desire to acquire Qualcomm's technology, a sector in which China was weak. The message, however, was clear – the fat of the land should be shared with the state.

The Party's overarching aim, though, has remained consistent: to ensure that the private sector, and individual entrepreneurs, do not become rival players in the political system in a way which threatens the single-party state. The Party wants economic growth, but not at the expense of tolerating and indeed nourishing any organised alternative centres of power. In the sessions on the Soviet Union ordered by Xi, officials studied not just the collapse of the Soviet Union but also its aftermath, when a new class of Russian oligarchs enriched themselves with the virtual theft of state assets. Chinese leaders watched in horror as the Soviet Union disintegrated and its assets were privatised. Having seen business threaten to take over the state in Russia, Beijing has been determined to make sure that the same disaster does not befall China.

The Party's efforts to place itself inside private companies have been, according to its own figures, very successful. One recent survey by the Central Organisation Department, the Party's personnel body, found that 68 per cent of China's private companies had party bodies by 2016, and 70 per cent of foreign enterprises.[71] Although these figures sound high, they don't match the targets the Party has set for itself. In Zhejiang, for example, Xi's old stamping ground and ground zero for the struggle between the CCP and entrepreneurs, the province set a target in August 2018 to have cells inside 95 per cent of private businesses. There was a need, the survey said, to retain the revolutionary spirit inside the companies as their ownership was handed on to the next generation.[72]

For a reliable benchmark about the power of the Party in China, you only need to listen to wealthy entrepreneurs hold forth on politics. Masters of the universe in their business domains, the otherwise all-powerful CEOs go to abject lengths to praise the Party. To take a few companies listed in a single article in the *South China Morning Post*, Richard Liu of e-commerce group JD.com predicted communism would be realised in his generation and all commercial entities would be nationalised. Xu Jiayin of Evergrande Group, one of China's largest property developers, said everything the company possessed was given by the Party and he was proud to be the party secretary of his company. Liang Wengen of Sany Heavy Industry, which builds earthmovers, went even further, saying his life belonged to the Party. 'They act as if they are being chased by a bear,' wrote Zhang Lin, a Beijing political commentator, in response to these comments. 'They are powerless to control the bear, so they are competing to outrun each other to escape the animal.'[73]

Jack Ma of Alibaba, the global face of Chinese entrepreneurship, has always managed to strike a quirkier and more independent stance than his fellow billionaires. 'Be in love with the government. But don't marry them,' he once memorably said.[74] Ma's pithy aphorisms at home and abroad were mostly a plus for his business, but they had a downside. Ma's high profile made him vulnerable. If there was a presidential election in China tomorrow, Ma might win, one of his former business partners told me, only half joking, adding that it was a dangerous position to be in. In September 2018, Ma announced unexpectedly that he would step down from a day-to-day role in the company the following year. Ma said he wanted to focus on education and philanthropy. An equally plausible reason for his resignation, the former business partner said, was Ma's fear that his power and popularity had made him a target of the Party. Ma has been in the Party since the 1980s, although his membership was not declared until late 2018, after his retirement announcement, in an article in which the *People's Daily* complimented him for his contributions to reform.[75]

Whether or not some entrepreneurs were intent on taking him on, Xi pre-emptively took the fight to them. In 2017, the Xi administration began a campaign to rein in swashbuckling business leaders, starting with some of the corporate chieftains who had become the standard-bearers for aggressive Chinese dealmaking overseas.[76] There was no clear pattern in the approach the government took. Some business leaders were forced out of overheated commercial sectors such as real estate. Others were told to pull back from offshore forays either because their high profile was an embarrassment for Beijing or because the government was trying to stop capital flight. Some, such as Wu Xiaohui, the chairman of Anbang Insurance Group, went the way that communist members who fall foul of the system do, vanishing without explanation into the party's detention system. Only months earlier, Wu had been leading negotiations to spend US$14 billion on hotels in the United States, before the deal collapsed. In May 2018, the authorities announced Wu had been sentenced to 18 years in jail for fraud and embezzlement.[77]

China's three dominant internet companies, Baidu (a search engine), Alibaba (e-commerce) and Tencent (messaging and gaming), known collectively as the BAT, have all felt the government's wrath. In 2018, Tencent lost US$200 billion in its market capitalisation after regulators stopped approving new online games, pushing the company out of the world's top ten companies ranked by their share market valuation.[78] The rapid growth of the BAT companies and their dominance of the internet in China has given them an outsized economic status.[79] But their political value is just as important, as they have become indispensable to China's surveillance state. With the mountain of data they generate, the BAT trinity are in effect turning into a real-time, efficient and privately run intelligence platform. In that respect, they are ideal private companies. They both drive economic growth and also buttress the political system.

Foreign CEOs, too, have come under pressure to give the Party a larger role in their firms. Again, this is not a trend that started with Xi. Walmart, which famously won't allow unions in its US stores, has had party cells in its companies in China since at least 2006, and CCP-controlled unions even earlier. Under Xi, however, emboldened officials have pushed foreign firms harder to accommodate the Party and give its representatives a role in business decisions. Companies as diverse as the cosmetics giant L'Oréal to Walt Disney and Dow Chemicals in China now all have party committees and display the hammer and sickle on their premises. Executives from one European company were quoted as saying that party representatives had demanded to be brought into the executive committee and have the business pay their expenses.[80] Like Chinese entrepreneurs, foreign businessmen and women are trying to outrun 'the bear', not always with success. But the Party's persistent efforts to colonise the private sector have stoked a backlash of their own.

In late 2017, the EU business chamber in China formally complained about party organisations trying to extend their influence in their member companies, something they said would undermine the authority of their boards. 'A fundamental change of this nature . . . would have serious consequences for the independent decision-making ability of these [joint venture] companies,' the chamber said in a statement.[81] The chamber's argument, that an extension of the Party's functions had no legal basis, was met with indifference locally, at least in public utterances. 'When you are in Rome, do as the Romans do,' said Chen Fengying, an expert at the China Institutes of Contemporary International Relations, a foreign policy think tank. 'Foreign investors should respect local rules and regulations in China.'[82]

On one level, Xi has been untroubled by the backlash over his treatment of entrepreneurs. The idea that the private sector is being overly politicised is upside down, according to his world view. Business leaders should 'strengthen self-study, self-education and self-improvement,' he said in 2016. 'They should not feel uncomfortable with this requirement. The communist party has similar and stricter requirements on its leaders.'[83]

Later, in 2018, when the economy started to slow and the trade war was ramping up, Xi was much more pragmatic and solicitous. In November that year, he invited a select group of entrepreneurs, including Tencent's Ma Huateng (also known as Pony Ma), for a meeting in the Great Hall of the People. He wanted to reassure them that they were 'all part of our family'. At the same time, a surfeit of stories appeared in the official media urging banks to lend private firms more money.

Not all entrepreneurs were buying the new line. One businessman, Chen Tianyong, posted a lengthy rant on social media, which he titled 'An Entrepreneur's Farewell Admonition', explaining why he had left China. 'China's economy is like a giant ship heading to the precipice,' he wrote in a posting that was later taken down. 'Without fundamental changes, it's inevitable that the ship will be wrecked and the passengers will die.'[84]

CHAPTER FOUR

Buddha jumps the wall

In 2001, about a decade after the end of the Cold War and just as China was formally joining the global trading system, Henry Kissinger peered into his crystal ball. In his book *Does America Need a Foreign Policy?*, Kissinger pondered what might happen if Washington treated Beijing as a 'permanent adversary', an enemy that the United States had decided it was compelled to oppose because of its 'moral flaws'. Would it be smart, he wrote, for the United States to bunker down in Asia on that basis for another lengthy Cold War, deploying policies similar to those directed towards the former Soviet Union?[85]

On one level, Kissinger was prescient in imagining how such a policy might play out. He described a scenario in which the United States limited trade with China to non-strategic items, the phenomenon that we call 'decoupling' today. He suggested the United States would build up Japan's defences and increasingly treat Taiwan as an independent entity, both of which are true, after a fashion. Once he started to rattle towards a conclusion, however, Kissinger's crystal ball started to get foggy.

Kissinger argued Cold War-style policies would fail on multiple levels. Washington's ability to influence Tokyo would decline. The Korean Peninsula would turn into a 'tinderbox'. Washington's European allies such as Germany, sensing a vacuum, would rush to fill it with their own business deals. Regional nations with territorial ambitions might take the chance to expand their claims. 'Unless their own survival is directly and clearly threatened, the Asian nations will not be prepared to join a crusade that groups them together as were the nations of Europe in opposition to a single threat,' he wrote. 'A policy that is perceived as having designated China as the enemy primarily because its economy is growing and its ideology is distasteful would end up isolating the United States.'[86]

In a way, Kissinger was building a straw man with this line of argument. The United States has never attempted to build a NATO-like alliance in Asia against China. Arguably, it doesn't need one, as

Washington already has multiple treaty allies in the region. But Kissinger could turn out to be right in the end. Cold War analogies don't hold water, because Asian nations and the United States are all deeply enmeshed with China's economy in a way they never were with the Soviet Union. Regional nations, and indeed much of the West, may judge that their economic and diplomatic interests are best served by cutting a deal with China, leaving the United States to retreat to its own continent. Beijing knows that its presence in Asia is a geopolitical fact. For the United States, it is a geopolitical choice, one that the American public appears indifferent to defending, even if the Pentagon is not.

So far, however, the struggle to find a new order in place of a waning Pax Americana is not unfolding in the way Kissinger imagined. Regional nations from Japan to Australia and west to India are making no secret that they prefer Washington and its military to stay, and for their alliances to be refreshed. The reason is not an overbearing Washington insisting on maintaining primacy in Asia. Donald Trump, for one, couldn't have made it clearer that he would like the United States to abandon its traditional regional role. With the Pentagon and national security establishment sending the opposite message, that the United States is in Asia to stay, Washington has hardly been a beacon of dependability. But even amid the Trumpian chaos, US allies can't yet afford to give up on America. 'From time to time people put up a sign to say, "Yankee go home", but they do not seriously mean that,' said Singapore's Prime Minister, Lee Hsien Loong, in May 2019. 'If Yankee went home, they would be very sorry.'[87]

Certainly, the way Washington frames any contest with Beijing affects its allies' behaviour and choices. Some are hedging their bets like never before against over-reliance on the United States. Trump has already damaged Washington's relations with Europe and NATO. However, US policy is not the only determinant of the way countries, in Asia and elsewhere, are responding to the emerging new order. Rather, it is Beijing's behaviour, a factor that Kissinger, supposedly so conversant with China, barely weighed up in reaching his conclusions. In private, Kissinger has always been more hard-headed, telling one aide in the mid-1970s: 'When [the Chinese] don't need us, they are going to be very difficult to deal with.'[88] Old friends of China like Kissinger do not dare speak so frankly in public. But such sentiments are closer to the mark in explaining why the world has been reacting as much to Xi's China as it has to Trump's America.

Japan, to take one example, has not needed US pressure to reconfigure and strengthen its military.

Japanese Prime Minister Shinzo Abe has pushed for more military spending and greater US engagement himself, in response to rising threats from China and North Korea. Likewise, Australia's defence build-up and diplomatic agitation is as much a response to Beijing's assertiveness as Washington's weakness. Europe would love to work more closely with the United States on China trade policy, if only the White House would agree to cooperate. Even North Korean leader Kim Jong-un wants an insurance policy, cultivating Trump in part to balance against being dominated by his giant neighbour.

The transformation is most evident in the United States, with a haphazard, unstable Trump masking the increasingly solid foundations of an across-the-aisle hardening over China in Washington that started gingerly under Barack Obama. But the United States is not alone. Countries large and small around the world, from Australia to Germany, Canada to Malaysia and India to Kenya, are all rethinking and renegotiating their ties with Beijing. Difficult as it may be to see at home in China, the backlash against Xi Jinping is reaching full bloom overseas.

Big countries such as the United States are confronted by a once-in-a-lifetime challenge from Beijing. Small countries feel patronised and bullied. Neighbours worry about being marginalised.

Advanced industrial nations see China coming at them like an unstoppable train. All of these phenomena, bubbling under the surface for years, have burst into clear view during the ambitious Xi administration. Four countries – the United States, Germany, Australia and Singapore – in their own way provide case studies of what can go wrong with China, and the limits in pushing back.

The rivalry between the United States and China might be, in the words of one writer, the 'contest of the century'.[89] Yet in China, it is not hard to find people who echo Kissinger's view that the Americans are entering the contest driven by an inflated sense of moral superiority. Many Chinese depict Washington's anger as little more than the sour grapes of a country that cannot accept Beijing as a worthy peer. Nor, they argue, can Washington and its allies intellectually countenance a single-party state that is both successful and innovative. 'Western democracy has its problems. China's system has its problems, too,' said Hu Xijin, the sharp-tongued editor-in-chief of the *Global Times*, a nationalistic tabloid owned by the *People's Daily*. 'When we have problems, we will reform. But the West doesn't. They think everything [they do] is right.'[90]

There is something to this critique. Evan Medeiros, a key architect of Barack Obama's Asia policy in the US National Security Council, said the differences in the two political systems were an 'enduring source of distrust'. Chinese plans to tighten social control at home, he said, 'will only draw a sharper contrast with the United States'. The Chinese themselves have always seen the US system as inherently a threat, something that has always been reflected in the Party's propaganda guidelines. Equally, said Medeiros, 'there is no American political leader who will ever confer the legitimacy on the leader of the Communist Party, as the Chinese desire'.[91] In other words, both systems believe that the other is out to get them, and they are not entirely wrong.

The United States has always been able to overlook the moral failings of undemocratic systems when it has other interests in mind. Saudi Arabia, a theocratic state that was home to most of the September 11 bombers, is a case in point. Saudi Arabia has oil and is a rival of Iran, enough to persuade US presidents for decades to keep Riyadh tightly within its orbit. When Obama pushed back against this tradition, he was heavily criticised. But for the Chinese, it is laughably hypocritical for the United States to embrace a leader like Mohammad Bin Salman, the Saudi hereditary monarch who had a dissident slaughtered in his country's consulate in Istanbul in 2018, while still arguing that China's system lacks legitimacy. The difference, of course, is that while the Saudis will never challenge US dominance, China is doing just that.

To complicate matters, Americans are suffering a form of buyer's remorse with China. Washington, or at least much of its national security leadership, long believed that China would not buck the US-led global order because Beijing was such a beneficiary of it, either through a liberal trade regime or, for example, through the constraints the United States forced on rivals such as Japan. 'The United States has always had an outsize sense of its ability to determine China's course,' wrote Kurt Campbell and Ely Ratner, who both moulded Asia policy in the Obama administration. 'Again and again, its ambitions have come up short.'[92]

Washington's policy was based on a series of misjudgements, many of them quite reasonable at the time. Sandy Berger, Bill Clinton's late national security adviser, for example, depicted China in a June 1997 speech as being a divided country, 'with conflicting forces pulling in opposite directions: inward-looking nationalism and outward-looking integration'.[93] In truth, China's integration with the world has always been tailored to reinforce the nationalist narrative at home. In the words of analyst Tanner Greer, the 'let's-engage-China-to-make-it-a-responsible-stakeholder' policy was not as foolish as it is now portrayed. 'What should have been an opening gambit became a stale dogma,' said Greer. 'But it was a good strategy initially, one that terrified the Party leadership, so they took action to defeat it.'[94]

The Americans overrated their intrinsic attractiveness and strength as a benign, inclusive, unassailable superpower, especially in the post-Cold War glow of victory against the Soviet Union, another rival communist state. More to the point, they underestimated the Party's equal and opposite sense of its own exceptionalism. 'We wanted to believe that we could convince China that they would be better off with us in charge; that somehow, with more interaction and engagement, the Chinese would come to realise . . . [they] like to be told what to do by the United States,' said Oriana Skylar Mastro of Georgetown University. The United States also failed to understand, says Mastro, that China felt compelled to build up its military. China's leaders 'didn't feel safe surrounded by the US military, and ... their aspiration if they could at some point would be to reduce the US military presence in their periphery'.[95]

In his winning campaign for the White House, Donald Trump brilliantly lit up America's mood of a superpower scorned and under siege. In the Midwestern states that were pivotal to his victory, such as Michigan, Ohio and Pennsylvania, his complaint that China had been 'raping' America for decades through the use of industrial espionage and unfair trade resonated deeply. The complaints about China's role in hollowing out America's economy at home in turn solidified the foundation for his isolationist, anti-establishment foreign policy. Trump contended that foreigners were ripping off America twice, at home and abroad.

Trump's scorched-earth radicalism cleared the policy undergrowth in Washington in a way no conventional president ever could. Paradoxically, he also liberated much of Washington on China policy in the process. 'Everybody has now got a hunting licence. It is open season on China,' said Susan Thornton, who handled East Asia policy in Trump's State Department until being forced out by officials who wanted a harder line against Beijing.[96] But blowing up China policy doesn't mean there is agreement about what should take its place. 'The new consensus is that the old strategy is not working,' said Ely Ratner. 'But there's no consensus on what that means or what comes next.'[97]

It is too early to judge the enduring impact of Trump's presidency. Trump has never bothered with consistency, which is a good thing because his administration's China trade policies are riddled with contradictions. Trump is trying to bully US industries to pull production lines out of China, if not to bring them home, then at least to put them into friendlier countries. Alongside this policy of disengagement, Trump has been pressing the Chinese for greater market access, which will only tighten the two countries' economic ties. The split within the Trump administration between Steven Mnuchin at the Treasury, who wants a softer line with China, and the more uncompromising Robert Lightizer, the chief trade negotiator, is evidence of that. But however incoherent Trump's China policy might be, the US attitude to China has changed for good.

The short-term assumption about China has long been that it wouldn't take the United States head-on until it was ready. But the Trump administration has reversed this formula. The question is no longer what might happen when China confronts the United States. Rather, the United States is bringing on the confrontation itself, for fear of leaving the contest too late. The backlash elsewhere in the world, however, takes more explaining.

*

In 2014, when German Chancellor Angela Merkel asked Australia's then prime minister, Tony Abbott, what drove Australia's view of China, he replied with tongue only half in cheek, 'fear and greed'.[98] The same three words could sum up Berlin's view as well. Both Australia and Germany have China as their major economic partner and are more dependent than the United States on trade with Asia's giant, giving them every incentive to cultivate a stable political relationship. But both countries have, to differing degrees, done the opposite. They have picked political fights with China, potentially putting commercial ties at risk.

The debate in Australia over China has long been framed by a number of influential essays by Hugh White, a former bureaucrat and academic. White's thesis is summed up by the title of one of his books, *The China Choice*, which argued that Australia's refusal to acknowledge the strategic rivalry between the United States and China enabled policymakers to avoid the hard choices the two superpowers posed. The mantra that Australia does not need to choose between its security ally, the United States, and its trade partner, China, led to a policy of 'systematic duplicity'. White said that Australia, in trying to 'convince Washington that we are supporting it against China, and to convince Beijing that we are not', was fooling no one except itself.[99]

In framing the issue so starkly, White, an eloquent and prolific writer, also hamstrung the debate. White depicted the world in binary and often apocalyptic terms, a choice ultimately between war and peace, and even nuclear war at that. In doing so, he passed over all the ways Beijing has so adeptly played in the gap between conflict and the status quo. Beijing has been masterful in acting under the threshold of political and military conflict, from the way it weaponises money to influence foreign business and political elites to building and militarising large islands in disputed areas of the South China Sea. In doing so, Beijing has made enormous gains without coming close to firing a shot.

Australia's backlash came under Malcolm Turnbull. Before becoming prime minister in 2015, the former banker and businessman was more captured by the opportunity China offered than any threat the country posed. In speeches in 2011, he struck a tone not dissimilar to White's, playing up the need for balance between Beijing and Washington and arguing against a defence strategy based on the possibility of a naval war with China in the South China Sea. 'It makes no sense for America, or its allies, to base long-term strategic policy on the contentious proposition that we are on an inevitable collision course with a militarily aggressive China,' Turnbull said.[100] In office, he changed his views, disillusioned with China's protestations of goodwill in foreign policy and its hardball tactics in bilateral disputes. He also charged into battle in one of those gaps the Party had long been playing in, largely uncontested: its attempts to meddle in Australian politics. 'Foreign powers are making unprecedented and increasingly sophisticated attempts to influence the political process, both here and abroad,' he said in introducing legislation to combat foreign interference.[101]

In taking on China, Turnbull ran into multiple problems. The first was how to talk about both the influence and interference issue without stirring up racial divisions in a country where millions have Chinese ancestry. Australia is a modern multicultural country with deep xenophobic roots, making it perilous for a political leader to single out one ethnic group. The second was wrestling with Beijing's vocal supporters in the local business community and the universities, which are increasingly reliant on business from China. Only a few years earlier, James Packer, one of the country's richest men, had said Australia should be more 'grateful' to China for its purchases of commodities, as if Beijing was doing Canberra a favour by trading with it.[102] In the midst of the bilateral blow-up in 2018, Sydney University Vice-Chancellor Michael Spence accused Canberra, and by extension Turnbull, of 'Sinophobic blatherings'.[103]

The third obstacle is widespread ignorance among non-specialists of the Chinese political system, which means nearly every conversation about how it works requires a dose of adult education. Influence and interference operations? Isn't that just diplomacy? Doesn't everyone do that? The idea that the Party runs overt and covert operations among its diaspora is not a secret to anyone who has taken the time to study China. Xi Jinping is intimately familiar with such work, overseen by the United Front Work Department, a longstanding party body designed to win over or neutralise potential CCP opponents at home and leverage the diaspora abroad. Fujian province, where Xi served for more than a decade, is a focal point for such work because of its close interactions with Taiwan. In 2015, Xi made a high-profile speech on the need to intensify wooing of the diaspora. 'The more the merrier,' he said. 'We should not approach the matter as cooking fast food, but cooking a delicacy such as "Buddha Jumps Over the Wall".'[104] (The name refers to food so delicious that it could entice vegetarian monks from their temples to 'jump the wall' to eat a meat-based dish.)

In the end, Turnbull pushed through new legislation setting up a registry for agents of foreign governments, banning foreign political donations and requiring local organisations under the sway of outsiders to show their hand. These laws give the authorities the tools to force any covert activism on behalf of Beijing above ground, which will be healthy for Australian democracy. But building this new capability came at a cost. Bilateral relations soured, and bipartisanship over foreign policy threatened to crack in the bitter debate over China. The government was often ill disciplined and struggled to strike a consistent tone, which made its job harder. Turnbull and his ministers also bickered with big business, which backed a softer line with Beijing. For several months, Beijing cut off all ministerial-level contact with Australia. So far, the Chinese Government has mostly pulled its economic punches but some financial punishment is likely to be imposed in due course, once Beijing thinks it has Trump under control.

Hugh White has argued that Australia cannot develop clear and effective policies until it recognises that US primacy in Asia is over, and that China, one way or another, will become the dominant power. This worst-case scenario makes sense for a defence planner, once White's profession. Diplomatically, however, the opposite is true. If Australia concedes, in effect, that it is game over and that China will win, then policymaking becomes nothing more than a series of cascading concessions to the new hegemon. Australia's Pacific reset, an ambitious program to restore Australian influence among Pacific nations and counter China's growing presence announced in 2018, will be useless by definition. Why invest in such measures at all? Under Turnbull, Australia rejected White's advice and started to play in the gaps in between war and peace, just as China has been doing for years. If there was any lesson to be learnt, it was that Australia, at the start of a long and difficult journey, was barely equipped to make its way. Scott Morrison, who succeeded Turnbull, was greeted after he was elected in his own right in May 2019 by snarky comments from the Chinese state media, reminding him of that. 'Australia's next Government still has a long way to go if they want to repair China–Australian relations,' the *Global Times* editorialised.[105]

A Berlin-based scholar described Australia's trade with China as 'primordial', which was his mordant way of distinguishing the more sophisticated, but equally lucrative, business that Germany did with the mainland.[106] Australia sells resources; Germany sells its high-quality engineering and design skills, embodied by its top-of-the-range autos. German companies have made huge bets in China over the past three decades and continue to do so. Those bets have paid off big time. Even though German carmakers, like all foreign companies, were forced to enter 50:50 joint ventures with local government-owned partners, meaning half of the profits flowed one way or another back to the Chinese state, their investments have still succeeded way beyond early expectations.[107] Audi sells three times as many cars in China as in the United States; Mercedes-Benz and BMW more than double. China now accounts for 40 per cent of Volkswagen's global sales. 'The future of Volkswagen will be decided in the Chinese market,' said Chief Executive Herbert Diess in January 2019. German auto companies are investing heavily in electric cars in China, a new industrial front that Beijing is trying to lead.[108]

The bountiful business relations between Germany and China have often been described as a marriage between two engineering cultures. Germany took the lead, while China learnt at the feet of the master. Berlin, along with Brussels, may have complained for years about market barriers in China. But the profits for the car companies and other industrial conglomerates, such as Siemens, which has about 80 joint ventures and wholly owned companies in China, far outweighed the grating difficulties of working through bureaucratic obstacles on the ground. Like Australia, the overwhelming sentiment in Germany until recently was 'let the good times roll'.

That sentiment changed decisively in 2015 with the publication by Beijing of the 'Made in China 2025' report, which laid out a roadmap for the party state to march its economy up the value chain over the next decade. The report laid out in detail the industries China was targeting and the precise market share it wanted domestic enterprises to garner. In German eyes, this wasn't just a case of the student surpassing the teacher. It was a recipe for the student sidelining the teacher altogether. Many in German politics, business and academia started to arrive at a similar conclusion to a now chastened and alert US establishment: that China was more a hostile power than a partner. 'People started to think that they don't want to compete with us,' said Sebastian Heilmann, a prominent China specialist in Germany. 'They want to replace us.'[109]

When Chinese firm Midea proposed buying Kuka, a German robotics maker, in late 2016, Angela Merkel was annoyed to discover that the government had no mechanism to block the deal short of declaring it a national security threat. Kuka was the kind of middle-sized industrial firm with world-class technology that has formed the backbone of Germany's economic strength. The surprise purchase of a US$9 billion stake in Daimler-Benz by Geely, a private Chinese carmaker, in early 2018 also made headlines. On another front, Berlin has been annoyed by Beijing's efforts to cultivate smaller EU states, in effect undermining European unity. We respect 'one China', German leaders have told their Chinese counterparts. Why can't you respect 'one Europe'? Among the broader populace in Germany, Beijing's fury over activists in Germany waving Tibetan flags at football matches involving the Chinese national junior team cut through with popular opinion in a way that a trade issue never could. The Chinese talked about 'mutual respect', the Germans about 'free speech', two concepts that could not be reconciled. A high-level football exchange, which had been sealed between Xi and Merkel, was called off.

If there was a single moment that made a lasting impression with the political and business elite about Xi's China, it was when the Mercator Institute for China Studies (Merics), a Berlin-based think tank, released a report on 'Made in China 2025'. The 2016 report was a wake-up call by itself, detailing how the Chinese leadership systemically intervened in domestic markets to benefit Chinese enterprises and to disadvantage foreign competitors. 'In essence, Made in China 2025 aims for substitution,' the report says. 'China seeks to gradually replace foreign with Chinese technology at home, and to prepare the ground for Chinese technology companies entering international markets.'[110] Most importantly, the report detailed how the sprawling Chinese state, at central and local levels, was committed to subsidising this industrial upgrade and protecting local companies that received their support.

The report included an illustration, a simple heat map that displayed in a loose grid which foreign countries had most to lose from competing head-on with China. For all the words in the report, which was targeted at specialists, the heat map was something politicians and business leaders could grasp immediately. Closest to the sun was Germany, along with South Korea, which both looked like they would melt in the face of the blaze coming out of Beijing. 'Germany did not get nervous until the business community started to get nervous,' said Mikko Huotari, Deputy Director of Merics. 'They have realised the golden era is over.'[111]

Germany's change of heart resulted in concrete changes in policy, all of them requiring Berlin to expend heavy political capital in Brussels. In late 2017, the European Parliament passed new laws giving the continent greater anti-dumping powers, a measure designed to slow the flow of cheap Chinese goods into the continent. Brussels is also readying an EU-wide screening process to review foreign investments on national security grounds. The process is modelled on the opaque committee headed by the US Treasury that Washington uses to screen foreign takeovers. With such a measure in place, it is doubtful that the Chinese takeover of another German company like Kuka would be approved.

The bigger impact of the backlash in Germany against China may be beyond Berlin's borders. Berlin is now talking more to Canberra, swapping experiences and strategies. Canberra is caucusing with Washington and both are talking more with Tokyo about their shared China angst. Ottawa reached out to its Western partners after its citizens were detained in late 2018 in China in the Huawei case. In turn, Wellington looked for support among like-minded countries around the time New Zealand's relations with Beijing began to fray. Even with Trump in the White House, the conversation about China is creating what the Germans like to call an emerging alliance of multilateralists. Washington's landmark trade report on China in 2018, for example, approvingly cites the Merics report on China 2025. All of these countries want to coordinate more with nations in Asia on the same issues. But as the example of Singapore shows, making common cause with Southeast Asia is harder.

Google 'Singapore's relations with China' and the search prompts four other questions: 'Is Singapore part of China?'; 'Is Singapore a US ally?'; 'Is Singapore a Chinese country?'; and 'Is Singapore safe?'. The questions neatly encapsulate the different directions that Singapore has always been pulled in, a small nation determined to build a distinct identity, slyly straddling the superpower and racial divides that surround it. Singapore's success is in no small part due to its founding father, Lee Kuan Yew, an authoritarian figure who turned a poor former British colony into a modern city-state. Although its population is about three-quarters ethnic Chinese, Lee was clear from the start that Singapore would be its own place. Cultural affinity with China does not mean allegiance to China, he said in 1965, the year Singapore gained independence.[112] Lee was referring to neighbouring Malaysia but the same applies to Singapore. China's rise, however, is making Singapore's balancing act harder to pull off.

Singapore always had an outsize role as a model for post-Mao China. It displayed, as one commentator wrote on Lee's death in 2015, how 'economic prosperity could be achieved under crisply efficient one-party rule, immunized from the temptations of liberal democracy'.[113] Doubtless, Singapore exaggerated its importance as a model for China. Beijing borrowed from lots of countries and systems. But Singapore's positioning as a bridge between East and West helped secure good ties with Beijing, even closer relations with Washington, and the kind of tight links with Taiwan that few other countries could pull off. Beijing has tried to seduce Singapore by stressing their shared Chinese heritage. Singapore's reply has always been: we are not Chinese; we are Singaporean.

Singapore's deft positioning, however, is under stress. China's economic power has been sucking Singapore in, just as it has done to every other country in the region and beyond. The political system has begun to wobble in the wake of Lee's passing, with a feud breaking out between his surviving sons and their families amid tensions over the transition to a new generation of leaders. Beijing has also been turning up the heat politically, hauling Singapore over the coals in disputes over the South China Sea and Taiwan in recent years. Beijing has little patience for Singapore's close ties to Washington and Taipei, and the city-state's emphasis on ASEAN unity.

For Singapore too, America has become as much part of the problem as the solution. Many senior officials in Singapore despaired of what they regarded as Barack Obama's emphasis on engaging China on climate change, which they complained came at the expense of security policy and a stronger line on regional territorial disputes. If Beijing could ignore Washington's protestations and roll over Manila after an international tribunal ruled in the Philippines' favour over Chinese claims in the South China Sea, why should Singapore stick its neck out? But if Obama failed to stand up to Beijing, Singapore's complaint about Trump is the opposite, that he is too confrontational. 'To actively avoid taking sides actually also requires actively not being pressured to take sides,' said Singapore's Prime Minister, Lee Hsien Loong. 'Unfortunately, when the lines start to get drawn everybody asks, "Are you my friend or not my friend?"'[114]

The debate in Singapore was exemplified by an acrimonious split between two of the country's most experienced national security bureaucrats. In July 2017, Kishore Mahbubani, a senior diplomat and academic, wrote an article describing the backlash against Qatar for its meddling in various Middle

Eastern disputes. 'Qatar ignored an eternal rule of geopolitics: small states must behave like small states,' he noted. 'The best time to speak up for our principles is not necessarily in the heat of a row between bigger powers.' Mahbubani's article, which, in not so many words, was saying that Singapore should not criticise China over the South China Sea in particular, provoked an explosive reaction.[115]

Bilahari Kausikan, a former head of the Foreign Ministry, called his one-time colleague's article 'muddled, mendacious and indeed dangerous'. Kausikan said he wasn't so stupid as to not recognise the 'asymmetries of size and power', but that did not mean Singapore had to grovel to build relationships: 'I don't think anyone respects a running dog.'[116]

A year earlier, in 2016, Kausikan had laid the ground for his argument with a coruscating public critique of Beijing's efforts to corral Singapore and other Asian states through bullying and manipulation. 'China does not merely want consideration of its interests,' he said. 'China expects deference to its interests to be internalised by ASEAN members as a mode of thought; as not just a correct calculation of ASEAN interests vis-à-vis China but "correct thinking" which leads to "correct behaviour". Foreign policy calculations are subject to continual revision; correct thinking is a permanent part of the sub-conscious. This differentiates Chinese diplomacy from the diplomacy of other major powers and represents a melding of Westphalian diplomatic practice with ancient Chinese statecraft.'[117]

In the short term, Kausikan had the better of the debate. In August, Huang Jing, a prominent Chinese–American political scientist and one of Mahbubani's senior colleagues at Lee Kuan Yew School of Public Policy, was expelled from Singapore for 'knowingly' interacting with intelligence agencies from an unnamed foreign country. By the end of the year, Mahbubani was no longer the Dean of the prestigious school. But the storm masked the real trend, of Singapore modulating its statements on the South China Sea and other issues. Singapore increasingly feels it has to find ways to accommodate Xi's China. As one senior Australian diplomat has noted, 'they have seen the weapons of torture' and responded accordingly.[118]

Conclusion

The United States, Australia, Germany and Singapore have all tried to push back against Xi Jinping's China in their own way. The United States is the flailing superpower, finally finding its feet on China even as it goes through something akin to a political nervous breakdown. Australia, or at least its national security bureaucracy, is in a steely mood but battling to find options that give it traction outside of the traditional alliance system. Germany has lost its sense of complacency but worries about the commercial downside of taking too tough a line. Singapore is struggling to find a way to operate in China's shadow and maintain its autonomy. The United States is, at least, an empire unto itself. The other three countries do not enjoy the luxuries of a superpower. They are stuck between empires.

It is little wonder they worry as much about Washington as they do about China.

Smaller countries that cross China know they will pay a price. Beijing cut tourism to South Korea and harassed its businesses inside China after Seoul agreed to deploy a US anti-missile battery. Norway had its salmon imports blocked for awarding the Nobel Peace Prize to the dissident, Liu Xiaobo. Mangoes from the Philippines were left to rot after Manila won an international court case against Beijing on the South China Sea. In 2019, Chinese buyers shied away from Australian coal and stopped buying Canadian canola. 'When China is angry with you, if you are any country other than the United States, they punish you . . . It's how China manages things,' said David Mulroney, the former Canadian Ambassador to Beijing, speaking in the wake of the detention of his country's citizens in the show-down over Huawei. 'Maybe we need a conversation among countries who've been victimised by this, about how we collectively push back.'[119]

Those conversations are now happening with increasing regularity. But for all their value, they have failed to come up with anything like a Plan B – in other words, a way to maintain a rules-based system in the absence of a strong and engaged America. Although many Australian officials and politicians think they are starting to emerge from the worst of the debate over China, in truth Australia has yet to face a genuine test. The public in Australia and elsewhere will only feel pressure when tensions with China move out of the politically esoteric realm of influence debates and into managing an economic rupture. Once Australians start losing their jobs because of Chinese economic sanctions, it is far from certain that the country and its leaders will hold their ground.

Beijing has already diluted ASEAN unity, peeling off Cambodia and Laos, which can be relied on to take China's line. Those gains, in turn, help Beijing in its bigger and more difficult battle in maritime Asia, where it still feels hemmed in by the United States and its allies. In the meantime, Beijing is making great strides in securing and strengthening its western flank with the Belt and Road Initiative. Once the shine comes off the Xi Jinping–Vladimir Putin relationship, there will be tensions with Russia, which is gradually being marginalised by China in Eurasia. One of the Initiative's prime partners, Pakistan, is a strategic asset but a difficult friend. Yet overall, to use an old Soviet phrase, the correlation of forces is moving China's way.

There is a perverse benefit for the Party in a back-lash from overseas as well, as it matches decades of state propaganda that foreigners are out to get China and contain its rise. The leadership in Beijing certainly fears facing a united front of foes in the West, collectively marshalling resources to push back against China. As a result, Beijing is deploying well-worn tactics, isolating and punishing some countries while accommodating and rewarding others. Internally, however, at least in the short term, Trump's hardball tactics will help Xi. 'Outside pressure of this sort would not drive a wedge between China's rulers and ordinary Chinese people,' wrote US scholars Michael Swaine and Ryan DeVries, referring to a Cold War-style containment policy. 'Instead, such a strategy would likely spook many Chinese citizens into rallying around government-sponsored nationalism, validating deep-seated suspicions that so-called hostile foreign forces seek to prevent China's resurgence.'[120]

The rally-around-the-flag sentiment produced by the showdown with Trump over trade and technology has dampened criticism of Xi for now. It may even help some of his advisers, such as Liu He, the vice-premier in charge of the US trade negotiations, persuade Xi to adopt more liberal economic policies. But for the moment, fighting foreigners has prompted a spike in nationalistic fervour and a determination to back national champions in technology. 'For us, this is a real "people's war",' said *Xinhua* in May when Trump increased tariffs on hundreds of billions of dollars of Chinese goods.[121] Trump initially rattled the Chinese leadership. But his compulsion to constantly up the ante means he overplays his hand and alienates potential allies in Europe and Japan, and inside China itself. With Beijing, rather than creating space for a deal, Trump's tactics may in fact close one off.

Many Chinese in the Obama era viewed American power as an empty throne. In its place, they now see a mad king fronting for a hostile American empire. In such circumstances, the benefits of engagement from Beijing's perspective are diminishing. 'Even if a trade deal with the United States is still possible, some in the Chinese leadership are now starting to ask, why bother?' wrote Kevin Rudd, Australia's former prime minister, in May 2019. 'Perhaps it's better, in China's view, to cut its losses now and get ready for the next Cold War.'[122]

There is no foreseeable scenario under which Beijing will back away, either rhetorically or in practice, from its territorial claims in Taiwan and in the South and East China Seas. As Xi Jinping told the then US Defence Secretary Jim Mattis in June 2018, China will not give up 'even an inch' of its territory, which includes its expansive maritime claims and a large land area disputed with India.[123] Within the Chinese system, any leader who stepped back from these claims would be committing political suicide. The internal sensitivity of the territorial issue helps explain the bellicose way Beijing handles these disputes outside of its borders. China constantly schools its Asian neighbours on its red lines in territorial disputes, all the while rapidly building up its military capability and regional diplomatic sway to entrench them. With the possible exception of Vietnam, smaller countries have taken to either submitting or swerving in the face of Beijing's pressure.

Yet it is far from game over, if history is any guide. Total capitulation in international relations is rare. Behind the scenes in Beijing, there has always been recognition that it was dangerous for China to bully its way to regional domination. 'The history of contemporary international relations does not provide any precedent of a large country successfully bringing to its knees another country,' wrote Wang Jisi, formerly of Peking University, and for many years an informal government adviser. Wang pointed to America's experience in Vietnam and more recently Afghanistan, where its vastly superior military firepower couldn't drag it out of a military and then political quagmire.[124] Wang was writing in 2014. Such strategic humility is rare in Beijing these days, either because the Chinese themselves have become cockier or because the country's diplomats fear being caught out of step with the temper of Xi's times. Nonetheless, the point stands. Beijing cannot bully its way to superpower status without engendering a strong pushback from other countries, which is exactly what is happening.

The opacity of Beijing's internal politics makes judgements about disruption inside China difficult. As a leader, Xi is unique in post-revolutionary party politics in not having any identifiable rival or successor, largely because he has ensured that none have been allowed to emerge. Even Mao Zedong had rivals, which of course resulted in his instigating violent campaigns and reprisals to remove them. Xi has so far done the same, without the brutality of mass mobilisation campaigns. Victor Shih, a US China specialist, was doubtless right when he said that the threshold for some kind of 'intra-party uprising' against Xi was very high: 'He would need to commit a catastrophic mistake that jeopardises the continual rule of the Party for his potential enemies within the Party to rise up against him.'[125] For the moment, Xi's only real rival is offshore, in the form of Donald Trump, which is why so many small-l liberals in China have grown to admire and like the US president.[126]

The idea that Xi is literally 'president for life', however, as he is often referred to in the wake of the

2018 abolition of term limits, in all likelihood will be proved wrong. From mid-2018, Xi was already facing a public backlash on economic policy, where it has always been safest for Chinese to speak out. Xi has a legion of critics on foreign policy as well, who believe he has overreached and left the way open for the United States and others to bind together on issues ranging from trade and technology to military and strategic influence in East Asia. Finally, the abolition of term limits summed up the rage that many influential officials and scholars felt about their country's leader. In one decision, Xi confirmed his critics' view that he was an unrepentant autocrat willing to take China backwards in the service of his agenda.

Wang Jisi was one of the few scholars to admit that the US backlash was at least in part of Xi's making. 'If we are looking for the cause, it was the change in Chinese policy that led to adjustments in US policy towards China,' he said in late 2018, referring to issues such as Beijing's harder line on Taiwan and the Party's tightening grip on politics and society. 'US policy has changed because China has changed.'[127] Another scholar, Yan Xuetong, generally regarded as hawkish, blamed the United States for the collapse in bilateral relations in a 2019 article. But he obliquely criticised Xi as well. 'The recent popularity of strongmen in major states will also devalue the strategic credibility of foreign policy and only increase the uncertainty of international politics in the coming decade,' Yan said. 'Such leaders' personal interests may often overwhelm national interests, including strategic credibility.'[128]

That even famous Chinese scholars have to guard their words about Xi so carefully is a reminder of the fear his power still strikes through the system. But just as it is difficult to anticipate where any challenge will come from, it is equally hard to see how Xi's supremacy in domestic politics can be sustained. In the face of criticism, especially over economic policy, Xi has displayed a pragmatic streak since mid-2018. He has talked up the private sector, agreed to tax cuts to spur growth and also scaled back the ambitious Belt and Road Initiative. 'Though Xi has earned a reputation for ideological rigidity and the single-minded pursuit of his agenda, he has in fact exhibited capacity for tactical policy adjustment,' according to Cheng Li and Diana Liang at the Brookings Institution.[129]

Yet Xi shows no sign of modifying his core objectives or being willing to share power, which means his opponents will have to take increasing risks to force him to do so. Other factors that remain out of Xi's control will also weigh against him. China's slowing economy and rapidly declining demographics can obviously be leveraged to argue in favour of maintaining tight authoritarian controls. But they are much more likely to work against Xi in future. The same applies to China's tightening fiscal situation. Beijing's ability to throw money at every problem, such as bailing out cash-strapped local governments, will only get harder. By the time of the next party congress, due in late 2022, the issue of succession should return with a vengeance.

In the short term, the trade showdown with the United States seems to have pushed the widespread anger at Xi's authoritarian ways back underground. When those tensions resurface, as they inevitably will, China's domestic tensions will flow out into the world in unpredictable, volatile ways. China's domestic insecurity, after all, feeds rather than restrains its desire to assert itself overseas. Even more reason, then, for Western countries to stand in solidarity when China overreaches. That does not mean replacing cooperation with confrontation at every turn. It simply means competing with China, speaking openly about its actions and standing up to it when necessary. Such policies might come at a cost. But to do otherwise will allow Beijing to pick off smaller nations such as Australia one by one. That would leave not just regional nations isolated. Eventually, the United States would be on its own as well.

Endnotes

1   Chris Buckley and Adam Wu, 'Xi Jinping Opens China's Party Congress, His Hold Tighter than Ever', *The New York Times*, 17 October 2017.

2   Uri Friedman, 'Trump Calls Out Election Meddling – By China', *The Atlantic*, 26 September 2018.

3   Zhang Chulin (Chunlin Zhang @clz030857), 'The arrest of Canadians was politically motivated? So was that of Meng', Twitter, replying to @KennedyCSIS, 27 January 2019.

4   Demitri Sevastopulo, 'Why Trump's America is Rethinking Engagement with China', *Financial Times*, 15 January 2019.

5   Jacob Pramuk, 'Chuck Schumer Urges Trump to "Hang Tough on China" after Latest Tariff Threat while Other Top Democrats Are Quiet', CNBC, 6 May 2019.

6   Andrea Worden, 'China Deals Another Blow to the International Human Rights Framework at its UN Universal Periodic Review', China Change, 25 November 2018.

7   Ian Johnson, 'A Specter Is Haunting Xi's China: "Mr
    Democracy"', *The New York Review of Books*, 19 April
    2019.

8   Jason Subler and Kevin Yao, 'China Vows "Decisive" Role
    for Markets, Results by 2020', Reuters, 12 November 2013.

9   Nicholas Kristof, 'Looking for a Jump-Start in China',
    The New York Times, 5 January 2013.

10 Ben Blanchard, 'Xi Jinping's Journey from China Party
    Elite to Party Leader', Reuters, 15 November 2012.

11 Damian Grammaticus, 'China's New President Xi Jinping:
    A Man with a Dream', BBC News, 4 March 2013.

12 See Shi Jingyue, 'Xi Jinping zai guang dong kao cha shi
    de jiang hua', in *Zhong gong ban mi mi bao gao: Xi
    Jinping nan er meng: jiu dang*, 1st edition (New York:
    Mirror Media Group, 2014); also see a discussion of this
    issue in Matt Schiavenza, 'Where Is China's Gorbachev?',
    The Atlantic, 14 August 2013. Figure based on World
    Bank data from 1991 to 2013.

13 See Suisheng Zhao, 'The Ideological Campaign in Xi's
    China: Rebuilding Regime Legitimacy', *Asian Survey* 56,
    No 6 (2016), p.1171.

14 See Schiavenza, 'Where Is China's Gorbachev?'.

15 Quoted in a book review by Benjamin Nathans, 'The
    Real Power of Putin', *The New York Review of Books*,
    29 September 2016.

16 Wendy Wu and Choi Chi-yuk, 'Coup Plotters Foiled: Xi
    Jinping Fended Off Threat to "Save Communist Party"',
    South China Morning Post, 19 October 2017.

17 Lily Kuo, 'Wang Quanzhang: China Sentences Human
    Rights Lawyer to Four Years in Prison', *The Guardian*,
    29 January 2019.

18 'China's Xi Says Political Solution for Taiwan Can't Wait
    Forever', *Reuters*, 6 October 2013.

19 Damian Grammaticas, 'Admiration Lingers for Bo Xilai in
    China's Chongqing', BBC News, 20 September 2013.

20 Shi Jiangtao, '"No Separation of Powers": China's Top
    Graft-Buster Seeks Tighter Party Grip on Government',
    South China Morning Post, 6 March 2017.

21 Alan Beattie and Richard McGregor, 'China Faces Fresh
    Tasks on Trade', *Financial Times*, 11 December 2006.

22 David Lague and Benjamin Kang Lim, 'How China Is
    Replacing America as Asia's Military Titan', Reuters,
    23 April 2019.

23 Minnie Chan, 'Top Chinese General in Graft Probe
    Commits Suicide in Beijing', *South China Morning Post*,
    28 November 2017.

24 Gerry Shih, 'In China, Investigations and Purges become the
    New Normal', *The Washington Post*, 22 October 2018.

25 *The Wrath of Heaven* by Fang Cheng (pseudonym) was
    published in 1995 and quickly banned in China. This
    quote comes from Richard McGregor, *The Party* (London;
    New York: Penguin, 2010).

26 Stephan Collignon and Vittorio Allegri, '"Tigers and
    Flies": The Ancient Roots of Xi Jinping's Anti-Corruption
    Campaign' (Master's thesis, University of Trento, 2016),
    p.5, http://www.academia.edu/31543681/_Tigers_and_
    Flies_The_ancient_roots_of_Xi_Jinpings_anti-corruption_
    campaign.

27 Wang Qishan, 'Fa hui xun shi jian du zuo yong, zhu li
    quan mian cong yan zhi dang', Politics.people.com.cn,
    21 August 2015, http://politics.people.com.cn/n/2015/
    0821/c1024-27494330.html [accessed 21 March 2019].

28 'New Progress in the Legal Protection of Human Rights
    in China (5)', *People's Daily*, 15 December 2017,
    http://en.people.cn/n3/2017/1215/c90000-9305147-5.html.

29 In theory, Xi's family could have been investigated for
    corruption, but not Xi himself. Any investigation of any
    senior official has to be approved at one level up. In
    the case of a member of the Politburo inner circle, such
    as Zhou Yongkang, when there is no higher collective
    authority, approval would have to come from his
    colleagues in the leadership, with an informal nod from
    retired elders. In the case of the general secretary himself,
    there is no one more senior and, therefore, no way to
    approve an investigation into him.

30 'Xi Jinping Millionaire Relations Reveal Fortunes of Elite',
    Bloomberg News, 29 June 2012.

31 Ibid. The story, by Michael Forsythe, was removed by
    Bloomberg, although it can still be read on the company's
    terminals. It can also be read here: https://www.sopasia.
    com/wp-content/uploads/2013/10/HKBU-SOPA-2013-_
    Program-Booklet.pdf.

32 Michael Forsythe, 'As China's Leader Fights Graft, His
    Relatives Shed Assets', *The New York Times*, 17 June 2014.

33 David Barboza, 'Billions in Hidden Riches for Family of
    Chinese Leader', *The New York Times*, 25 October 2012.

34 The position of China's diplomats around this time was
    instructive. Publicly, they denounced and denied the reports
    of their leaders' wealth. Privately, they insinuated that, far
    from painstakingly researching their articles, the foreign
    reporters had the information delivered to them in a
    document dump by political rivals from inside the Chinese
    system. In saying this, they seemed to confirm that this was
    how politics was being played at the top in China, with rival
    clans gathering dossiers on their enemies and then releasing
    the information for maximum effect in internal struggles.

35 The US equivalent of Xi's campaign would have seen
    the top generals on the joint chiefs of staff arrested; the
    head of Exxon Mobil and Chevron, along with many of
    their senior executives, detained; and the governors of
    Pennsylvania and Texas behind bars, along with the former
    chief of staff to the president, the number two and three
    leaders at the FBI and the CIA, the head of the Federal
    Communications Commission, the operational chiefs
    (that is, the deputy leaders) of the banking and insurance
    regulators, and senior scholars at the Brookings Institution.

36 Personal communication with the author, February 2019.

37 'Lu shi, faxue boshi deng 59 ren lianming zhi quanguo
    renda gongkaixin [Open letter to the National People's
    Congress by 59 people, including lawyers and Juris
    Doctors]', Human Rights in China, 11 August 2017,
    https://www.hrichina.org/chs/gong-min-yan-chang/lu-shi-
    fa-xue-bo-shi-deng-59ren-lian-ming-zhi-quan-guo-ren-da-
    gong-kai-xin-guan.

38 Gao Hongming, 'Wo dui "zhongguo gongchandang
    zhengfa guongzuo tiaoli" de fumian yinxiang [My negative
    impressions of the CCP regulation on political and legal
    work]', Boxun News, 21 January 2019, https://www.
    peacehall.com/news/gb/pubvp/2019/01/201901210632.shtml.

39 See 'Zhejiang sheng wei changwei, sheng jiwei shuji, sheng
    jian wei zhuren liujianchao zhuanfang [Interview with Liu
    Jianchao, head of the Zhejiang Provincial Commission
    for Discipline Inspection]', People's Daily, 15 December
    2017, http://fanfu.people.com.cn/n1/2018/0110/c64371-
    29756258.html.

40 See Zhang Rongchen, 'Zhunque bawo "dang zheng
    fengong" gainian [An accurate grasp of the concept of
    "party and government division of labour"], People's
    Daily, 10 April 2017, http://theory.people.com.cn/
    n1/2017/0410/c40531-29198863.html.

41 Xi Jinping, 'Zai qingzhu quanguo renmin daibiao dahui chengli 60 zhounian dahui shang de jianghua [Speech at the celebration of the 60th anniversary of the founding of the National People's Congress]', *China Communist Party News*, 5 September 2014, http://cpc.people.com.cn/n/2014/0906/c64093-25615123.html.

42 Quoted in Gordon Watts, 'Breaking Down the Walls Strangling China's Private Sector', *Asia Times*, 9 October 2018.

43 Nicholas Lardy, *The State Strikes Back: The End of Economic Reform in China?* (Washington, DC: Peterson Institute for International Economics, 2019), p.2.

44 Huang Yasheng, 'Why More is Actually Less: New Interpretations of China's Labor-Intensive FDI', William Davidson Institute Working Paper No 375, 14 August 2001.

45 Gabriel Wildau, 'The State Strikes Back, by Nicholas Lardy', *Financial Times*, 27 January 2019.

46 Angus Grigg, 'No Such Thing As a Private Company in China: FIRB', *Australian Financial Review*, 16 January 2019.

47 David Sanger, Julian Barnes, Raymond Zhong and Marc Santora, 'In 5G Race with China, US Pushes Allies to Fight Huawei', *The New York Times*, 26 January 2019.

48 Hans Von Der Burchard, 'Trump's Envoy Urges Europe to "Link Arms" against China', *Politico*, 6 February 2019.

49 Henry Paulson Jr, 'The United States and China at a Crossroads', Remarks at the Bloomberg New Economy Forum, Singapore, 6 November 2018.

50 Frank Tang, 'China's Pro-Market Economist Wu Jinglian Warns of "State Capitalism" Dangers', *South China Morning Post*, 21 January 2019.

51   Nectar Gan, 'Economist Zhang Weiying Slams "China Model" that "Inevitably Leads to Confrontation with the West"', *South China Morning Post*, 26 October 2018.

52   Kinling Lo, '"Made in China 2025" All Talk, No Action and a Waste of Taxpayers' Money, Says Former Finance Minister Lou Jiwei', *South China Morning Post*, 7 May 2019.

53   See transcript of speech, 'Xiang Songzuo: The Pitiful State of the Chinese Economy', *Asia News*, 21 January 2019, http://www.asianews.it/news-en/Xiang-Songzuo:-The-pitiful-state-of-the-Chinese-economy-46023.html.

54   Ashley Feng, 'We Can't Tell if Chinese Firms Work for the Party', *Foreign Policy*, 7 February 2019.

55   Michael Forsythe and Dexter Roberts, 'China's Next Boss Has Some Capitalist Cred', Bloomberg, 27 January 2012.

56   Embassy Beijing, 'Zhejiang Party Secretary Touts Economic Successes and Work Towards Rule of Law at Ambassador's Dinner', WikiLeaks Cable: 07BEIJING1840_a, dated 19 March 2007.

57   Ibid.

58   Xi Jinping, 'Liyong min zi da you qianli [The great potential for using private capital]', Xuanjiangjia [71.cn], 22 January 2013, http://www.71.cn/2013/0122/702262.shtml; '15 nian qian, xijinping wei zhejiang liu xia yi fen "zhanlue zichan" [Fifteen years ago, Xi Jinping left Zhejiang with a "strategic asset"]', *People's Daily*, 20 July 2018, http://politics.people.com.cn/n1/2018/0720/c1001-30160045.html.

59   Michael Collins, participant in panel discussion (moderator: Bob Schieffer), 'Scheiffer's Series: China's Rise', Center for Strategic and International Studies, 20 March 2019, which can be viewed on YouTube at https://www.youtube.com/watch?v=8StW3wqW0kg.

60   Jack Ma, speaking on a panel on 'The Future of Equality and Opportunity', closing plenary session of the annual meeting of the Clinton Global Initiative, 30 September 2015, which can be viewed on YouTube, starting at about 14 minutes in, at https://www.youtube.com/watch?v=l7Be_6NEPQE.

61   Wendy Leutert, 'Firm Control: Governing the State-Owned Economy Under Xi Jinping', *China Perspectives*, No 2018/1-2, November 2018.

62   See Lea Shih and Kerstin Lohse-Friedrich, 'CCP Membership Structure: Centralised Leadership – Heterogeneous Party Base', Merics *China Monitor*, 19 July 2017, https://www.merics.org/en/china-monitor/content/3511.

63   Daniel Rosen, Wendy Leutert and Shan Guo, 'Missing Link: Corporate Governance in China's State Sector', Asia Society Report in collaboration with the Rhodium Group, November 2018, p.32. A number of measures are taken from this paper. Thanks to Wendy Leutert for her research in this area.

64   Quoted in Rosen, Leutert and Guo, 'Missing Link: Corporate Governance in China's State Sector', p.21.

65   See 'Guoyou zichan baogao zhidu jianli jinian 10 yue jiang shouci shai guozi jiadi [State-owned assets reporting system to shed light on state-owned resources for the first time this October]', *Xinhua*, 18 January 2018, http://www.xinhuanet.com/fortune/2018-01/18/c_1122275054.htm.

66   Ana Swanson, 'US Joins Europe in Fighting China's Future in WTO', *The New York Times*, 29 November 2017.

67   'Gaige kaifang 40 nian, fei gong jun dai ni xi shu fei gongyouzhi qiye dangjian fazhan lichen he jingyan [Development history and experience of party-building in non-public enterprises]', *Xinhua*, 23 May 2018, https://mp.weixin.qq.com/s/hUdUgl8QuVg6cmrf6aWKnQ.

68 Xiaojun Yan and Jie Huang, 'Navigating Unknown Waters: The Chinese Communist Party's New Presence in the Private Sector', *China Review* 17, No 2 (2017).

69 'Qianghua shifan daidong tuijin liang ge fugai [Strengthening demonstrations to promote two coverages]', *Gongchandang yuan wang* [*Communist Party Network*], 31 July 2018, http://news.12371.cn/2018/07/31/ARTI1533019460323426.shtml.

70 Andrew Browne and Rebecca Blumenstein, 'China Internet Regulator to Qualcomm: "We Should Make Money Together"', *The Wall Street Journal*, 10 September 2014. Lu Wei was later arrested for corruption.

71 Zhang Lin, 'Chinese Communist Party Needs to Curtail its Presence in Private Businesses', *South China Morning Post*, 25 November 2018.

72 Fei gongyouzhi qiye dangjian [Non-public enterprise party-building], 'Qiao heiban! Zhejiang liang xin dangjian gongzuo zhongdian luo zai zhexie fangmian! [Pay attention! These are the key aspects of Zhejiang's two new party-building activities!]', *WeChat*, 27 August, 2018, https://mp.weixin.qq.com/s/_EMht5dBEkapwPcVc_7tWA.

73 Zhang, 'Chinese Communist Party Needs to Curtail its Presence in Private Businesses'.

74 'Jack Ma on Alibaba's Relationship with the Chinese Government', CBS News, 20 January 2018, https://www.cbsnews.com/video/jack-ma-on-alibabas-relationship-with-the-chinese-government//.

75 'Alibaba's Jack Ma is a Communist Party Member, China State Paper Reveals', Reuters, 24 November 2018.

76 See Richard McGregor, 'China Takes On Its New Tycoons', *The Wall Street Journal*, 13 October 2017.

77 Maggie Zhang, Xie Yu and Jun Mai, 'Anbang's ex-Chief Wu Xiaohui Sentenced to 18 Years Behind Bars for US$12 Billion Fraud, Embezzlement', *South China Morning Post*, 10 May 2018.

78 Tom Hancock and Louise Lucas, 'Tencent Hit as China's Freeze on New Video Game Titles Continues', *Financial Times*, 15 October 2018.

79 It is worth noting that Baidu is the weakest of these three companies, with a search engine that lags well behind Google's.

80 Michael Martina, 'Exclusive: In China, the Party's Push for Influence Inside Foreign Firms Stirs Fears', Reuters, 24 August 2017. The company was not named in the article.

81 European Union Chamber of Commerce in China, 'Chamber's Stance on the Governance of Joint Ventures and the Role of Party Organisations', 3 November 2017.

82 Chen Qingqing, 'Foreign Firms Concerned over Party Building', *Global Times*, 29 November 2017.

83 See Xi Jinping's address to the Fourth Session of the 12th National Committee of the Chinese People's Political Consultative Conference, 4 March 2016, http://cpc.people. com.cn/xuexi/n1/2016/0310/c385475-28188107.html. Also quoted in McGregor, 'China Takes On Its New Tycoons'.

84 Li Yuan, 'China's Entrepreneurs Are Wary of the Future', *The New York Times*, 23 February 2019.

85 Henry Kissinger, *Does America Need a Foreign Policy? Toward a Diplomacy for the 21st Century* (London; New York: Simon & Schuster, 2001), p.135.

86 Ibid.

87 Lee Hsien Loong, Prime Minister of Singapore, Keynote Address at the 18th Asia Security Summit, IISS Shangri-La Dialogue, Singapore, 31 May 2019, https://www.iiss.org/-/ media/files/shangri-la-dialogue/2019/speeches/keynote-

address--lee-hsien-loong-prime-minister-of-singapore--
provisional.ashx.

88 Personal interview with the late Richard Solomon, March
    2015.

89 See Geoff Dyer, *The Contest of the Century* (New York:
    Knopf, 2014).

90 See Zheping Huang, 'Global Times Editor Hu Xijin on
    US–China Relations, Press Freedom in China, and the June
    4 Protests', Quartz, 9 August 2016.

91 Evan Medeiros made his comments in 'The China Debate:
    Are US and Chinese Long-term Interests Fundamentally
    Incompatible?', at the Brookings Institution, Washington,
    31 October 2018, which can be viewed on YouTube,
    starting at about 13 minutes in, at https://www.youtube.
    com/watch?v=liERzupvRa-o&t=9849.

92 Kurt Campbell and Ely Ratner, 'The China Reckoning',
    Foreign Affairs, March/April 2018.

93 Remarks by Samuel Berger, Assistant to the President for
    National Security Affairs, Council on Foreign Relations,
    New York, 6 June 2019, https://www.mtholyoke.edu/acad/
    intrel/bergchin.htm.

94 Personal conversation with Tanner Greer, based on a tweet.

95 Oriana Skylar Mastro, speaker at the *Foreign Affairs*
    January/February Issue Launch: 'Who Will Run the World?
    America, China, and Global Order', Council on Foreign
    Relations, 30 January 2019, https://www.cfr.org/event/
    foreign-affairs-januaryfebruary-issue-launch-who-will-run-
    world-america-china-and-global-0.

96 Sevastopulo, 'Why Trump's America is Rethinking
    Engagement with China'.

97 Jenny Leonard, 'Don't Count on US–China Trade
    Relations Warming Up Anytime Soon', Bloomberg
    BusinessWeek, 5 April 2019.

98 John Garnaut, '"Fear and Greed" Drive Australia's China Policy, Tony Abbott Tells Angela Merkel', *The Sydney Morning Herald*, 16 April 2015.

99 Hugh White, 'America or China? Australia Is Fooling Itself That it Doesn't Have to Choose', *The Guardian*, 27 November 2017.

100 Malcolm Turnbull, '"Same Bed, Different Dreams" – Asia's Rise: A View from Australia', Speech to London School of Economics, 5 October 2011.

101 'Australia Passes Foreign Interference Laws amid China Tensions', BBC, 28 June 2018.

102 Damon Kitney, 'We Should Be a More Grateful Friend to Beijing, Says James Packer', *The Australian*, 15 September 2012.

103 'University of Sydney Vice-Chancellor Criticises Government's "Sinophobic Blatherings"', ABC *RN Breakfast*, 31 January 2018.

104 'Xijinping tan tongzhan gongzuo: benzhi yaoqiu shi da tuanjie da lianhe [Xi Jinping discusses the work of the United Front], *China Communist Party News*, 22 November 2017, http://cpc.people.com.cn/xuexi/n1/2017/1122/c385476-29660701.html.

105 Quoted in 'Chinese State Media Says Shock Federal Election Victory Will Impact China–Australia Relations', ABC News, 20 May 2019.

106 Personal communication with the author, 9 February 2019.

107 The 50:50 rule is now being slightly eased.

108 Thank you to Michael Dunne for these figures. See also 'VW, China Spearhead $300 Billion Global Drive to Electrify Cars', Orocobre, 17 January 2019.

109 Personal communication with the author, 31 May 2019.

110 Jost Wübbeke et al, 'Made in China 2025: The Making of a High-tech Superpower and Consequences for Industrial Countries', Merics Papers on China No 2, December 2016, p.7.

111 Interview with Mikko Huotari, Deputy Director of Merics, 21 February 2019.

112 See 'Transcript of an Interview Given by the Prime Minister, Mr Lee Kuan Yew, at NZBC House on 11th March, 1965', National Archives of Singapore, http://www.nas.gov.sg/archivesonline/data/pdfdoc/lky19650311a.pdf.

113 Chris Buckley, 'In Lee Kuan Yew, China Saw a Leader to Emulate', *The New York Times*, 23 March 2015.

114 Lee Hsien Loong, Prime Minister of Singapore, Keynote Address at the 18th Asia Security Summit, IISS Shangri-La Dialogue, Singapore, 31 May 2019.

115 Kishore Mahbubani, 'Qatar: Big Lessons from a Small Country', *The Straits Times*, 1 July 2017.

116 'Minister Shanmugam, Diplomats Bilahari and Ong Keng Yong Say Prof Mahbubani's View on Singapore's Foreign Policy "flawed"', *The Straits Times*, 2 July 2017.

117 'Bilahari Kausikan's Speech on ASEAN and US–China Competition in Southeast Asia', 3rd IPS–Nathan Lecture, 30 March 2016, recorded in *Today*, 31 March 2016, https://www.todayonline.com/world/bilahari-speech-us-china.

118 Personal communication with the author, January 2019.

119 'A Fraying Canada–China Relationship', *The Agenda with Stephen Paikin*, 5 February 2019: comments can be viewed on YouTube, starting at about 24 minutes in, at https://www.youtube.com/watch?v=AOtsxkROAjo&t=1586s.

120 Michael Swaine and Ryan DeVries, 'Chinese State Society Relations: Why China Isn't Trembling and Containment Won't Work', Carnegie Endowment for International Peace, 14 March 2019.

121 See Ben Westcott, 'Chinese Media Calls for "People's War" as US Trade War Heats Up', CNN, 14 May 2019.

122 Kevin Rudd, 'Trump Hands China an Easy Win in the Trade War', *The New York Times*, 29 May 2019.

123 Phil Stewart and Ben Blanchard, 'Xi Tells Mattis China Won't Give Up "Even One Inch" of Territory', Reuters, 27 June 2018.

124 Wang Jisi, 'The Simultaneous Slide in Chinese–American and Chinese–Japanese Relations Is Not Beneficial', 1 September 2014.

125 Isaac Chotiner talks with Victor Shih, 'A Political Economist on How China Sees Trump's Trade War', *New Yorker*, 23 May 2019.

126 The writer Zha Jianying talks about this phenomenon in 'Sinica Live with Zha Jianying: Dealing with the Troublemakers', *Sinica* (podcast), 21 February 2019, https://supchina.com/podcast/sinica-live-with-zha-jianying-dealing-with-the-troublemakers//.

127 Zhao Lingmin, 'Fang Wang Jisi: meiguo fadong maoyizhan bushiweile likai zhongguo [An interview with Wang Jisi: A trade war announced by the US does not aim at decoupling]', *FT Zhongwen* [*Financial Times* Chinese], 16 October 2018.

128 Yan Xuetong, 'The Winner of China–US Conflict Rides on National Leadership', *East Asia Forum*, 2 April 2019.

129 Cheng Li and Diana Liang, 'Rule of the Rigid Compromiser', Brookings, Spring 2019, https://www.brookings.edu/articles/rule-of-the-rigid-compromiser/.

Acknowledgements

Thank you to the Lowy Institute's Executive Director Dr Michael Fullilove and Director of Research Alex Oliver for pushing this project. Sam Roggeveen and Lydia Papandrea provided invaluable editing. For help with research, I would like to thank Cai Qiuxian, Maxim Jones, Cherry Zhang, Eleonore Wang and Lai Wenqi. Any errors remain, sadly, my own.

Lowy Institute Papers

LOWY INSTITUTE PENGUIN SPECIALS